The Easy Break

A Radically Simple System for Better Putting, Chipping, and Bunker Play

Large Print Edition

Todd Kolb

T-Interactive

For you, the golfer who loves the game and is determined to play at your highest level...

...whether that means competing in high school, shooting your age in retirement, or winning your first major.

May this book show you what you're capable of.

Contents

Bonus Content — vii
Introduction — ix

Part One
Putting

1. Putting: The Objectives — 5
2. Putting: The Foundation — 15
3. Putting: The Motion — 27
4. Putting: The Practice — 33
5. Putting: The Mistakes — 45
6. Putting: The Situations — 57
7. Putting: A Recap — 63

Part Two
Chipping

8. Chipping: The Objectives — 75
9. Chipping: The Foundation — 81
10. Chipping: The Motion — 89
11. Chipping: The Practice — 99
12. Chipping: The Mistakes — 115
13. Chipping: The Situations — 127
14. Chipping: A Recap — 139

Part Three
Bunkers

15. Bunkers: The Objectives	155
16. Bunkers: The Foundation	161
17. Bunkers: The Motion	167
18. Bunkers: The Practice	171
19. Bunkers: The Mistakes	181
20. Bunkers: The Situations	191
21. Bunkers: A Recap	201

Part Four
Next-Level Short Game

22. Proper Expectations	215
23. Think Like a Champ	227
24. Practice Plans	241
25. Testing	247
26. Next-Level Short Game: A Recap	255
27. The Next Era of Your Golf Game	263
Free Bonus (Because You're an Insider Now)	267
Acknowledgments	269

Bonus Content

You're about to learn a lot of great information that will completely transform the way you think about your short game. To make sure all this game-changing insight is easy to understand, I've provided additional video instruction you can access at any time by visiting VLSGolf.com/EasyBreakTips or scanning the QR code below.

Bonus Content

You'll also get access to a lot of free bonuses at www.VLSCoaching.com/BookOffer. Follow that link to grab your bonus material or scan the QR code below.

If what you learn inspires you to go deeper with one-on-one coaching tailored to your game, visit www.VLSCoaching.com or email my team and me at:

Info@VLSGolf.com

To ensure a quick response, please put "Coaching" in the subject line.

Now let's get into the good stuff.

Introduction

Golf is more than a game.

But then, you know that. You're reading this book, which means this game matters to you. It's not just a time-killer.

Maybe you—like my daughter Emily—love golf for the relationships it's given you. Em grew up playing the game on local courses, on vacation, with family, and in tournaments. She now plays for Gustavus Adolphus College where she's currently a junior. Despite the major gains and victories she's enjoyed over a lifetime of dedicated practice, she'll still tell you what she loves most about golf is the friendships.

"There aren't a ton of girls who golf," she says, "so when you find them, you spend a lot of your

Introduction

time with them. All the girls I've met playing have become my lifelong friends."

Or maybe you're more like Angela Stanford, who's concluding her final year on the LPGA tour as I write this. For Angela, golf has always fed her competitive spirit. It provides a space where she can test her limits, push herself to excel, and rise to unexpected challenges.

"I played for Texas Christian University," she says, "and when I graduated, I had to make the decision: try for Q-School or do something else. I loved competing more than anything else, so I went to Q-School, got my card in the fall of 2000, and just never looked back."

My guess, though, is that you're like my student Barry. The game his mother introduced him to over half a century ago has given him a *lifetime* of gifts.

It's been a steady source of entertainment and fitness. It's an excuse to get out into the fresh air and sunshine. Through golf, he's been able to rise to new challenges, connect with old friends, and compete in tournaments. At one point, he even boasted a 3-handicap.

Now 73 years old, Barry can even say some of his greatest memories took place on the golf course, like when he made his first eagle as a teenager. His dad was there—as so many dads have been

Introduction

throughout golf history—as a witness and golf partner.

"We were on an uphill par 4, and I hit my second shot. We knew it was close, and I thought Dad was going to have a heart attack running up the hill. I think he was more excited about it than I was."

When I look at Barry, Angela, and Emily, I see what *I* love most about golf:

The game belongs to everyone. No matter your age or skill level, no matter where you live or who you play with, golf has the power to enrich your life, deepen your relationships, improve your health, and challenge you to push beyond your perceived limitations to unlock your true potential.

And the secret to golf's versatility can be found in the short game.

Not many people like to hear that. It's more exhilarating to imagine finding glory on the tee box —launching long, penetrating drives that seem to defy the laws of physics and leave onlookers with their jaws in the dust.

But let me tell you, power moves weren't going to help Barry when he returned to golf after surgery and an eight-year hiatus only to find that he could no longer play by a young man's rules.

Long drives weren't going to be the answer for Emily, either. As a lifelong witness to her golf game,

Introduction

I can tell you she's never been the one to hit it the farthest. But she's outplayed plenty of gals who can outdrive her, thanks to the way she performs around the green.

"It's taken a lot of pressure off my full-swing game," she says. "Which is nice because then I can just be a little more laid back when I'm playing, and that helps me play even better."

Even Angela, who built a solid professional career on a masterful long game, didn't achieve the ultimate goal of winning a major championship until she got serious about perfecting her short game.

Look around your local golf course. I can just about guarantee you'll see them—the "old guy" or "old gal" that can't swing out of their shoes anymore but still manages to show up golfers in their twenties. Or the young golfer who can't bring a ton of power to the tee but shoots alarmingly low scores simply because they've got their short game dialed in.

The only *real* goal of this game is to get in the hole in as few strokes as possible. It doesn't matter where you save your strokes. A 250-yard drive and a one-foot putt are worth exactly the same on your scorecard. And it will always be easier to lower your scores by fine-tuning your short game, whether you're 17 or 70.

Introduction

We treat the full swing like it's the prime example of athleticism in this game, but think of what it takes to excel around the green.

Strategy. Precision. Clarity. Patience.

These are the marks of a true athlete, and they're accessible to everyone at every phase of life.

If you're already familiar with my Vertical Line Swing System and my book *The Bad Lie*, you know my number one goal as a golf instructor is helping golfers find the solutions that work for them. *The Bad Lie* unveiled a new tee-to-green strategy that serves amateur golfers, especially the long-neglected senior player.

Now, in this book, I'm sharing revolutionary short-game techniques and unconventional methods designed to help *every* golfer lower their scores and revitalize their game. This book is for all players—the Barrys, Angelas, and Emilys.

This book is for *you*.

My goal is to not only provide simpler, more effective techniques, but to ignite a new love and appreciation for the short game. Along the way, you'll get to know a few of my students, including the three you've already met.

You'll also meet Claire. She's 65 and relatively new to the game, having picked it up in 2020 as a way to get outside and socialize safely at the height

Introduction

of the pandemic. A lifelong athlete, she took to the game immediately.

"I love being outside in nature on the course," she says. "It gives you a great opportunity when you're on trips to see beautiful areas, and it's a wonderful destination sport. And it's really great for friendships. I've made new golf friends, and some of my long-time friends are getting into it, too. My husband and son are really getting interested, so we're all having fun playing together."

Claire's long-term vision for her golf game involves hitting up courses all over the country with her husband and eventually sharing her love for golf with her now-two-year-old granddaughter.

Then there's Walt, who turned 80 as I was writing this book. Like Barry, Walt fell in love with the game at a young age and grew up playing with his dad and friends on a local course. He wasn't able to play as much during his working years, but he's been getting out to golf regularly in retirement. The game gives him a challenge to rise to.

"That's kind of my makeup as a person," he says. "When I do something, I always try to improve and get better at it. Right now, I'm shooting about a 10-handicap and want to get down into single digits. I want to be consistently breaking 80. I do it now but not on a regular basis."

All five of these golfers have their own history

Introduction

with the game, their own reasons for loving it, and their own goals.

What they have in common is that they all envision a long, fulfilling future with golf... a future that involves time spent outdoors with the people they love, challenging themselves, and testing their limits. And they all know what you're about to discover: nothing—not age, injury, slow swing speeds, or even serious competition on a professional tour—can hold you back when you know how to dominate around the green.

As you'll soon see, Emily, Walt, Claire, Barry, and Angela have all taken huge steps forward with the very instruction you're about to learn. From nearly eliminating three-putts to feeling more relaxed in the bunker, they've discovered new confidence and sustainable success by sharpening their short game.

If you're ready to be able to say the same for yourself, you've come to the right place.

What This Book Covers and Why

I know how it is for amateur golfers. Ask for a little advice, and you get a thousand complex ideas thrown at you. No wonder it's so hard to keep a clear head as you get closer to the green.

Now, I can't deny it: by the time you set this

Introduction

book down, you *will* be equipped with a lot of new information. But I'm going to do all I can to simplify the process of retaining that advice and integrating it into your short game. In this book, you'll get clarity about what's *really* going on in each of your short-game shots, how to overcome common mistakes, and easy practice strategies for turning all that head knowledge into body knowledge so you don't *have* to think about it anymore. Along the way, you'll have plenty of recaps, checklists, and practice plans for building the techniques you learn into your game.

I paid close attention when readers of *The Bad Lie* told me which features of that book helped them practice their game, and you can bet I've doubled down on those features in this book.

I'm also skipping any insights that won't make a real difference in your short game. Once again, the goal is clarity, not more mental chaos.

And, of course, we'll cover three crucial short-game shots:

Putting

I think every golfer's been there. You hit a soaring drive, follow it with a solid second shot, and just like that, you're on the green in two. But you're nowhere near the hole. Your lag putting isn't di-

Introduction

aled in, your aim's a little off, and you three-putt it. Suddenly, those first two shots you were so proud of minutes ago are worthless. Painful, isn't it?

The fact is, the average golfer only hits a handful of greens in regulation, and when they do, very seldom are they left with a short putt. They're usually looking at a putt of at least 20 feet, and until you know how to make it into the hole in two from that distance, you'll be throwing away a lot of strokes.

Everything we discuss in this book's putting section is designed to help you take those strokes back.

Chipping

This is one of the most common shots in golf after putting and driving. But golfers have a particularly tough time practicing this one because every chip shot is different. The lie you're working with, how far you want the ball to carry, how far you want it to roll, the size of the green, whether you're navigating over a bunker... this isn't a one-solution-fits-all situation.

That's why you won't just learn the mechanics of a solid chip shot; you'll also learn how to adapt for a range of situations and gain deeper insight into the swing adjustments that can help you produce the shots you desire.

Greenside Bunkers

I've got to tell you something you won't believe. Tour professionals and high-level amateurs actually *prefer* the bunker over long greenside grass. If you can't imagine anyone feeling that way, you're probably among the many casual golfers who struggle to regain control of their round after landing in the sand.

In this book, you'll learn what the professionals know: this shot is completely manageable when you learn how to approach it like the unique situation it is. By the time we're done, you'll know how to get the ball out of the bunker every time. It may take a little practice, but if hitting bunker shots at your local course's practice green always feels a little risky, don't worry—I've got a tip for overcoming that hurdle, too.

Now, as a golf instructor, I know it's not enough to just throw some good advice your way. We need a system—a clear and simple strategy for building understanding, turning understanding into action, and transforming action into ongoing improvement.

Let's talk about what that looks like.

Introduction

Your Journey to a Better Short Game

Whether you've given it much thought or not, I bet you've got a vision for your golf game. Walt wants a single-digit handicap. Barry looks forward to continuously improving his game as he returns to the life waiting for him back home. Claire wants to build proficiency and confidence in a sport she expects will play a starring role in her travel adventures and family bonding.

Whatever goal you have in mind, this book is designed to get you cruising steadily toward your destination. We'll set you up with a clear route to follow and plenty of gas in the tank. We'll make sure we get those mirrors adjusted and check the dash for warning lights alerting us to any hidden issues that could cause catastrophe down the road. And of course, we'll get you building up speed as you hit the entrance ramp, ready to chase down your chosen destination.

The Putting, Chipping, and Greenside Bunkers sections all feature the following chapters:

Introduction

Objectives

This is where we pull out the map and lay out the best route. You'll learn what you're trying to accomplish in each shot, beyond obvious things like "I want to get the ball in the hole." These details will not only clarify your approach to the shot; they'll also help you strategize intelligently when unexpected obstacles arise.

Foundation

Now we're setting ourselves up for smooth, steady progress. We're gassing up the car, adjusting the mirrors, and picking our playlist. Or, in golf terms, we're learning how to set up the shot to accomplish the objectives we laid out in the previous section. Might seem pretty basic, but these key fundamentals determine the success of your shot.

Introduction

Motion

Time to get moving. Start the car and back out of the driveway. In this chapter, you'll learn how the body and club move together to create the perfect shot.

Practice

Go ahead and settle in behind the wheel. Take a few turns down surface streets as you make your way toward the freeway. Notice if you need to make any adjustments—shift your mirrors, move your seat, turn up the AC. In this chapter, you'll discover my best drills for implementing the lessons you've learned. With a little repetition, you'll settle into your new technique and feel more prepared to take those hard-earned skills to the golf course.

Introduction

Mistakes

Before you hit the freeway, you'll want to keep your eyes and ears open for all those lights and beeps alerting you to trouble. Never a good idea to start cruising when the trunk is ajar and the tire pressure is low. In this chapter, you'll get to know the most common errors amateur golfers make, how to identify them in your own game, and how to overcome them.

Situations

Now you're on the freeway entrance ramp, accelerating fast. This chapter takes you beyond the basics by giving you the right tools to tackle unique situations that can arise for the shot you just learned to master. This includes things like putting on aeri-

Introduction

fied greens, chipping uphill, and dealing with a fried egg lie in the bunker.

These chapters will get you well on your way to your goal. But I want to make sure you not only reach that destination but have plenty of fuel to venture beyond it. That's why you'll find an additional section: **Next-Level Short Game**. This is where you'll discover those next-level skills that separate kind-of-okay amateurs from champion players. You'll learn how to think like a champ, analyze your stats and performance effectively, practice strategically, and test your progress accurately.

You'll also get exclusive access to my **bonus Lost Chapter**, where you'll unlock the secret to overcoming the yips, hitting a super flop shot, mastering the 40-yard chip shot, and more. (Actually, you can grab that Lost Chapter right now at www.VLSCoaching.com/BookOffer or by scanning the QR code in the "Bonus Content" section.)

And along the way, you can visit VLSGolf.com/EasyBreakTips to see the concepts we discuss in this book demonstrated in short video lessons.

By the time you're done, you'll have everything you need to conquer the short game and meet your personal objectives. Best of all, you can count on these methods to work today and for as long as you play the game, because I didn't write this book for

Introduction

super fit athletes in their twenties. I didn't write it to help amateur golfers fantasize about pulling off the same complicated moves their favorite tour players have perfected.

I wrote it so that real-life, everyday golfers could enjoy bettering themselves and their game for years to come. I wrote it so you would have effective tools for creating more memories, whether that means surprising yourself with an eagle, breaking 80 for the first time, or being confident enough in your game to keep up with the younger generation, giving *them* the gift of golf memories that are full of *you*.

This game has so much more in store for all of us.

Let's seize the opportunity.

Part One

Putting

Golf is not an easy game. You can't expect a total transformation overnight.

That said, there *are* areas of the game where you can claim a quick win. I love pointing my students toward a fast victory because it shows them what's possible and boosts their motivation to push for more.

So when I met Claire, a high-handicap golfer who was relatively new to the sport, I zeroed in on the area where I knew a little extra practice would inevitably lead to lower scores:

Lag putting.

See, Claire's not yet in a place where she's effortlessly landing the ball on the green within tapping distance of the cup. Most casual golfers don't have that kind of control. But by mastering those long putts, she's now created a situation for herself where just getting it on the green is enough.

As she describes it, "I can be on the green and far away from the hole but then get the ball close to the hole on my first putt. And it probably saves me a stroke."

I *know* it does. That's why she points to lag putting as her short-game breakthrough.

For Barry, the big challenge has always been those three- to eight-foot putts. "That distance of a putt gets me anxious because I think I should make it," he says, "and more often than not, I don't."

Barry struggled with putting even when he was in his prime and playing competitively. While he's still plugging away at improving this aspect of his game, I'm thrilled to say he's seen a lot of improvement with the exact strategies you're about to learn.

As for Walt, he's been doing a dance many amateur golfers know all too well. "I used to have the most challenges with lag putts," he says. "Then I started getting better at lag putts and had real trouble missing three- to five-foot putts." He's struggled with aim on long putts and distance control on slopes. He's learned—as many lifelong golfers do—that a strong putting game is a moving target. We're not the same golfer decade to decade, year to year, or even day to day. And each time we improve in one area, we naturally want to advance to a new level of mastery.

Nevertheless, Walt is unlocking new control and consistency on the green using the techniques you're about to learn.

See, the putting lessons that follow are designed for simplicity and versatility. I'm not just here to teach you "good putting." I want to help you understand what makes a putt successful. I'm going to give you the tools you need to think through each putt with a clear head no matter how your skills evolve or what surprises the green has in store for you.

And the first step is to get clear on our objectives.

Chapter 1

Putting: The Objectives

You've got too many putting tips in your head. I can pretty much guarantee that.

From golf partners to YouTube videos to the voices you hear when you're watching golf on Sundays, you've collected so many scraps of putting advice I'm willing to bet it's nearly impossible to clear your head when you set up to the ball.

Head position, eye position, posture, body angles, clubface orientation, the shape of your stroke path, the direction of your target path, the break in the green, the distance between you and the cup... it's too much. Way too much. You'll never make more putts when you've got a mile-long, cut-and-paste checklist clogging your mental space.

So before I give you new tips to apply, I want to

help you clear the clutter. We're going to set aside the question of what actions you should take and focus first on what you're trying to achieve (aside from getting the ball in the cup). We're going to talk about what a successful putt looks like.

Get a solid grasp of that bigger objective, and it'll be easier to quiet the chaos in your mind when you're standing on the green with a shot at a birdie. You won't just know *what* to do; you'll know *why* you're doing it. You'll start making more putts consistently because you're not simply following a checklist; you're fulfilling a clear, definable goal.

And when unexpected challenges arise, you can do more than tap the ball and hope for the best. You'll be able to return to the three key objectives you're about to learn and tackle tough putting situations *strategically*.

Sounds pretty okay, right?

So let's get started.

The Three Objectives of Putting

Every good putt achieves three clear objectives.

Objective One: The putter face is square to the target line at impact. That one probably doesn't surprise you. The proper aim of the clubface is more crucial on the green than on any other part of the golf course.

Objective Two: The golfer delivers proper loft to the ball. Your putter already has a tiny bit of loft built into the face. All putters do. Standard putter loft is generally between two and four degrees, with three being the most common. That's the ideal amount for getting a decent roll on the ball and creating consistent distance control.

Objective Three: The stroke has the proper pace. You might also think of this as rhythm or cadence, but no matter what you call it, this aspect of your stroke determines your speed. If you struggle with distance control, you're not nailing your pace.

That's it—the three objectives you need to meet on every single putt if you want to make more putts consistently. Not too complicated, is it? So why don't you already have all this down?

Why You've Been Struggling to Fulfill These Objectives

Frankly, the most popular putting systems—the systems you've likely been taught—are harder than they have to be.

One common approach is the arc putting motion, in which you allow the club path to arc inwards slightly on the backstroke, then retrace that track as it moves back toward the ball, arcing in on the other side as you swing through.

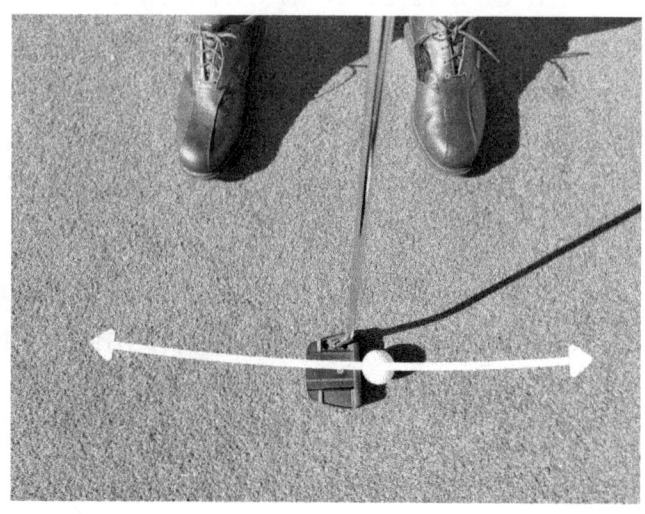

Now, there's a pretty significant downside here. **That arc motion means you'll have to deal with a *lot* of face rotation.** In order to consistently succeed at Objective One—the square putter face—**you'll need excellent hand-eye coordination and plenty of time to practice precision face orientation.** That's not realistic for most amateur golfers.

The other popular putting system is the "straight back and straight through" motion. This is when you keep the putter head on a perfectly straight path as you swing back and through.

The Easy Break

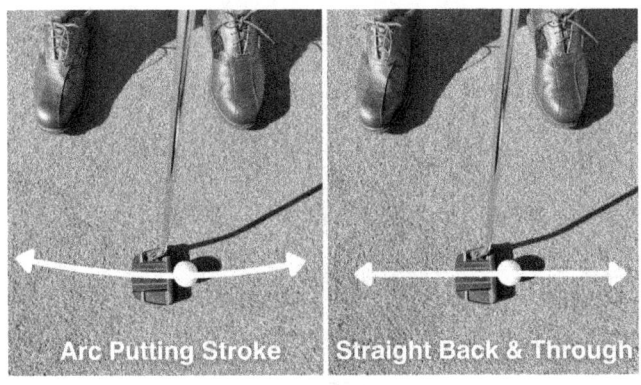

Now, it *seems* like it would be easier to maintain a square clubface with this approach. The problem is that we stand to the side of the golf ball, and we're typically 8-12 inches away from it. (More about the exact distance later). It's unnatural for the putter to move on a straight line from this position. The farther the putter head moves away from the ball, the more you have to extend the arms to maintain that straight line. **This is not natural.** You're constantly adjusting your body angles, which means there's a good chance you'll inadvertently change the clubface orientation and loft. Not to mention, anything that makes your body motion feel less natural is almost certain to mess up your touch and feel.

That's all three of our core objectives (clubface control, proper loft, and pace) compromised just by following a strategy widely respected as the gold standard putting motion and often taught to golfers like you. No wonder you're confused and struggling on the green.

Quick Side Note:

Your putter comes with features designed to help you meet those key objectives. This equipment has come a long way in recent years, including VLS's new G-Track, a fully adjustable putter I had the privilege of developing alongside one of the best designers in the game. I'll be honest; it was deeply gratifying to design a putter that could help amateur golfers modify their own club (legally!) to meet those three objectives more easily.

Now, I'll occasionally refer to the G-Track in the chapters that follow, both because the putter was designed around the principles we're discussing and because I know many of the folks reading this book will have one. Barry's got one. And Walt stopped missing those three-to-five-footers partly because of his. When golfers discover VLS Golf, they tend to go all in!

But rest assured, all the tips I share here work no matter what your preferred putter is. After all, every putter features elements created to help with your accuracy and speed control.

(By the way, if you're interested in checking out the G-Track, you can snag a discount at www.VLSCoaching.com/BookOffer. Consider it a "thank you" for trusting me to help you revitalize your short game.)

The ALL-Go Putting System

I developed the ALL-Go Putting System based on my observations over 30 years of coaching. This system combines the best of all putting styles, discarding everything that's over-complicated or requires an exceptional skill set.

Like the Vertical Line Swing, it's useful for golfers of all ages and skill levels but is designed specifically to help the experienced amateur golfer excel on their terms. The ALL-Go Putting System is easier on the body and easier to repeat. It requires less practice and demands less inherent talent. Most importantly, it actually gets results.

So what does it look like?

The ALL-Go putting system is essentially a hybrid of the arc putting motion and the straight-back-and-straight-through method. I took what works from those two systems and got rid of what doesn't.

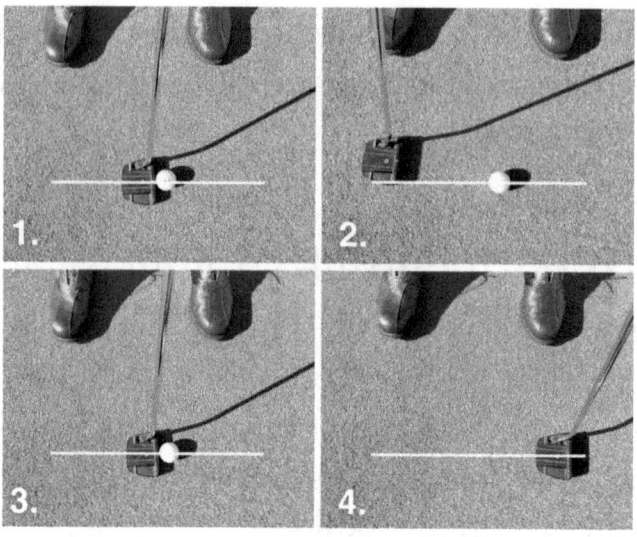

The concept is straightforward:

You want a slight arc on the backstroke, closing the clubface just a bit. This takes rotation out of the equation and makes it easier to deliver a square clubface on impact. You can see this in the photo in the top right square above. On the backstroke, the putter head moves slightly inward on an arc.

After that arced backstroke, you simply want to move the putter down the target line toward the cup. You can see this in the bottom right box: the putter head moves straight down the line through impact.

It might seem like you'd have to think harder about this putting approach, but once you learn the setup and get a quick primer on the motion itself, you'll discover that the ALL-Go Putting system is easier to master and repeat than anything else you've been taught.

So, let's set up the foundation that will help you drain more putts with less effort.

In Short...

- When you putt, you want to focus on three key objectives: delivering a square clubface, delivering the proper loft, and maintaining the proper pace.
- The two most common approaches to the putting stroke—the arc putting motion and the straight-back-and-straight-through method—make achieving these objectives more difficult than it has to be.
- The easiest and most effective technique for amateur golfers is a hybrid approach: slight arc on the backstroke and straight down the target line toward the cup. This is the ALL-Go putting system.

Chapter 2

Putting: The Foundation

By "foundation," I basically mean your setup. In this chapter, we're going to get your body, ball, and putter in the right place to achieve your three objectives without having to make any fancy maneuvers. Our goal, as always, is to create a putting motion that feels natural. That's the secret to control, repeatability, and success.

Just a heads-up: there's a lot of information here. But don't worry; you'll get a summary at the end of the chapter drilling everything down into clear, concise bulletpoints. You still might need to read this chapter a couple of times, though my best advice is to get on your feet as quickly as possible. The sooner you practice your new setup, the sooner you'll turn these concepts into a physical habit instead of a mental checklist.

Now, consistency is everything when it comes to your foundation. If you want to roll smooth, controlled putts every time, you've got to be able to set up to the ball the exact same way on every putt.

To that end, we're going to build a template—a physical guide you can take along to the practice green to make sure you're staying consistent.

Claire loves this template, by the way. See, long before she became a golfer, she was a dedicated tennis player. Still is. And if there's one thing she learned from decades of tennis, it's that excellence is something you earn by taking the time to get the details right… and get them right *consistently*.

Emily's a fan of the practice template, too. And as you can probably guess, growing up with me means she's used it a *lot*. "It really helps you recalibrate yourself and get back to the basics," she says.

That's exactly why we do it. Great putting begins with airtight fundamentals, and you're about to discover a technique for nailing those fundamentals now and maintaining them for years to come.

So grab **a Sharpie**, **an alignment rod**, **athletic tape**, and **your putter**, and let's get to it.

The Easy Break

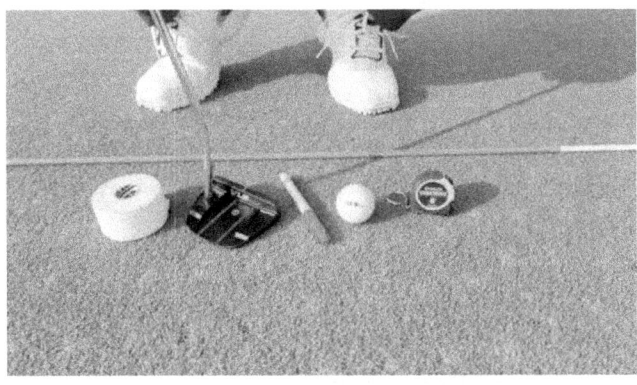

Distance From the Ball

In my experience, the ideal distance between the target line and your toe line is about the same as a standard putting grip (roughly 10 inches). Here's how you can find that distance every time you go to the practice green:

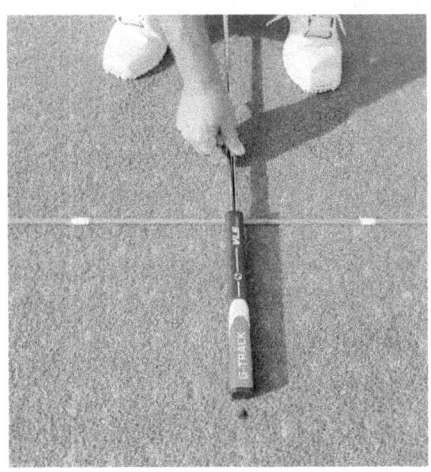

1. When you set up a practice putt, identify the spot where your ball will go. Draw a dot on that spot using your Sharpie. (Don't worry; you won't hurt the green.)
2. Lay your putter on the ground with the butt end against the dot with the shaft tracing a line toward your feet in setup position.
3. Slip the alignment rod underneath the putter at the bottom end of the grip. The rod should be perpendicular to the putter shaft and parallel to your target line.
4. Pick up the putter and place your toes against the rod. Your toes should now be roughly 10 inches (the length of a standard putter grip) from the ball.

The alignment rod now shows you where you should stand to maintain the correct distance from the ball. Easy, right?

Now let's continue building this template by adding stance width.

Stance Width

Your stance width is entirely up to you. Some golfers do best with a narrow stance. Others like to keep it wide. All that matters is that you feel stable and can move the putter the way you need to.

If you're not sure what your preference is, I recommend a shoulder-width stance. It's a little on the wider side, and I believe **it's generally better to err on the side of having a stance that's too wide rather than too narrow.** That's especially true if, like me, you don't have the same natural balance and stability you had ten or twenty years ago.

Whatever width you choose, it's important to keep it consistent. So we're going to build it into your practice template like this:

1. Position your toes along the alignment rod, finding the stance width that's comfortable for you.
2. Mark the position where the middle of your lead toes hits the alignment rod by wrapping a strip of athletic tape around the rod.
3. Do the same thing for the position of your trail foot.

You should now have tape at two points on your alignment rod showing you where your feet should be. Between this guide and the dot on the green, you'll be able to step out of position all you want and return to the exact same setup. When you want to practice from a different part of the green, just put a dot on your new ball position, use your putter grip to find the proper placement for your alignment rod, and start rolling more putts.

In time, you'll find the setup position naturally. You'll learn what the proper distance between you and the ball feels like. It'll be the same story for your stance width. The trick is to start with the guide so you *know* you're staying consistent and stick with it until the proper position becomes a habit.

Of course, these details are only the beginning of a solid setup. We still have more to discuss.

The Easy Break

Ball Position

This is another area where consistency pays off big time, so you're going to build proper ball position into your template to ensure you deliver the proper loft at impact. To do that:

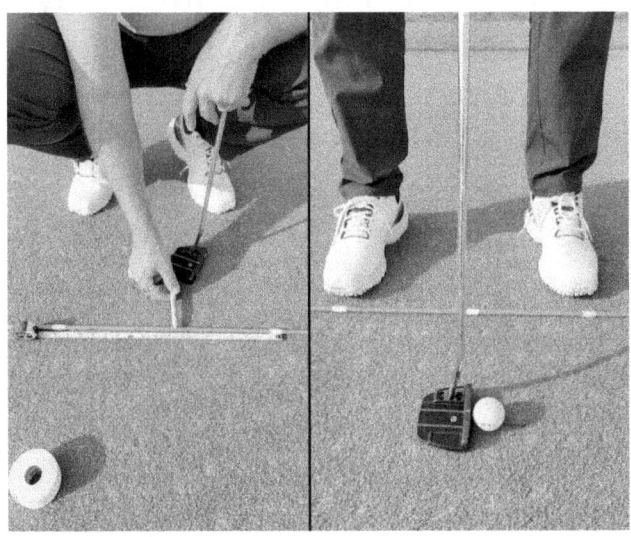

1. Measure your stance width as you have it marked on the alignment rod. Start at the outside edge of the piece of tape marking your lead foot position and measure to the outside edge of the tape marking your trail foot position.
2. Take the total measurement and divide it in half to find the exact center of your stance. For example, if your stance is 18

inches wide, the center would be 9 inches.
3. Wrap another piece of tape around the rod **slightly forward of center.** For example, if the center is 9 inches, I'd put a piece of tape at 8.5 inches from the lead foot. This is approximately where the ball will be positioned.

Now you've got a template that guarantees you'll get the ball in the right place, your feet in the right place, and stand the proper distance from the ball every time you practice. That alone is going to make a huge difference in terms of consistency.

Keep reading, though. We've got to talk about what the rest of your body should be doing at setup.

Eye Position

You've likely been told to get your lead eye directly over the golf ball at setup. That's actually not what you want for the ALL-Go Putting System.

As you stand over the golf ball, align your lead eye with the inside (trail side) of the golf ball. This eye position promotes a slight arc on the backswing and helps you keep the putter head moving down the line on the forward

The Easy Break

swing—the perfect putter head motion for the ALL-Go putting system.

Weight on the Feet

Eye Position: Lead Eye
Over the Inside of Golf Ball

Weight Distribution:
60% Lead - 40% Trail

Traditional putting advice would have you believe that you want an even distribution of your body weight in your putting stance. That is to say, you want to feel about 50% of your weight in your lead foot and 50% in your trail foot.

For the ALL-Go putting system, you actually want a little more weight on the lead foot—around 60-65%. You don't have to be exact about it. Just aim for a bit more than half. This extra weight on the lead foot will stabilize your body, resulting in a more consistent stroke and center-strike contact.

Grip

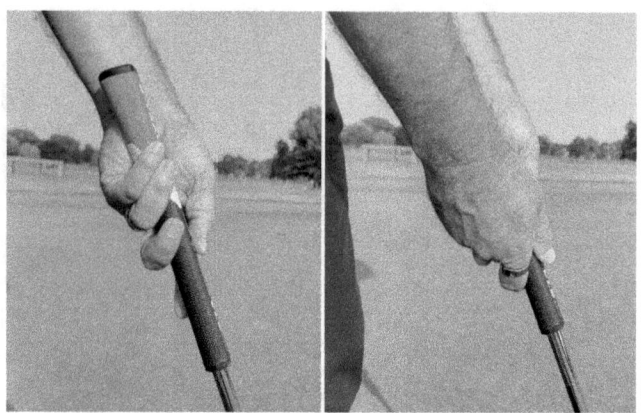

Putter runs through palms versus fingers
Thumbs point down toward the ground
Palms rotate slightly up toward the sky

To find the ideal putting grip, **hold the putter in the palm of your lead hand, with the handle running along the lifeline of your palm.** When you grip the putter in your palm, you'll find it's much easier to keep the putter face square and moving down the target line. This is because you're essentially stabilizing your wrists. If you hold the putter in your fingers, there's a greater chance your wrists will rotate and mess up your stroke.

Now, the key is to have the knuckles of your

The Easy Break

lead hand facing the target. **You should feel like you're pointing your thumb straight down the putter shaft and your palm is rotating slightly upward toward the sky.** Rotating your palms upward naturally pulls your elbows closer to your body, whereas an upward rotation creates a chicken wing effect. As for pointing your thumbs downward, that locks your wrists in—an especially big win if you struggle with twitchy muscles.

Once your lead hand is in position, **add your trail hand, sliding it up against your lead hand with your palm facing the target.** Your palms should now be facing each other in what we call a "neutral" position with both thumbs pointing down toward the ground.

Finally, **make sure the putter is in line with your forearms.** This is gonna help the putter travel along the same arc as your forearms for a more natural movement.

Now you've got the perfect grip, the ideal weight distribution, the proper eye and ball position, the stance width that suits you, and the correct distance between yourself and the ball.

In other words, you're in the perfect spot to execute a clean, smooth ALL-Go putting motion.

In Short...

- Position your feet a standard putter grip's length (roughly 10 inches) from the ball.
- Use whatever stance width works for you—just be consistent.
- Position the ball just forward of center in your putting stance.
- Align your lead eye with the inside (trail side) of the golf ball.
- Set up with 60-65% of your weight in your lead foot.
- Hold the putter in the palm of your lead hand, then add your trail hand with the palm facing the target. Make sure your palms are rotated upward, your thumbs point downward, and the putter is in line with your forearms.

Chapter 3

Putting: The Motion

You already know what the ALL-Go putting motion looks like.

It's a slight arc on the backstroke with a sightly closed clubface, then a down-the-line motion as you swing through.

This hybrid putting strategy is perfect for amateur golfers for three simple reasons:

1. It requires very little face rotation to deliver a square face on impact.
2. It makes it easy to deliver proper loft every single time.
3. You'll have no trouble repeating this motion correctly on a regular basis. I'm guessing that fact alone makes it a

winner over everything else you've tried. At least, that's the case for pretty much all the amateur golfers I've taught this method to.

The only question is, how do you pull this off? How do you turn this concept into a physical motion that feels natural?

We're going to use a system I call "Aim, Lock, Load, and Go."

Aim

You probably don't even need my help to figure this step out, but I'll offer it anyway in the interest of being thorough.

You're going to use that little line on the top of your putter (if you have a G-Track, it's actually one white line and two red lines) to set up your aim. Center that line behind your ball and point it in the direction you want the ball to start.

Easy enough, right?

Lock

Once you've set up your aim, check your grip to make sure it's working along the lifeline of your lead hand. This is going to help you maintain a proper arc in your backswing.

Load

Now you're going to load the putter by **slightly moving the grip end of the putter toward the target.** We are talking just a fraction here; don't overdo it.

You might notice that this de-lofts your putter face a bit. **That's a good thing**. The vast majority of amateur golfers inadvertently *add* loft at impact. By loading the putter and de-lofting the face in your setup, you offset that almost inevitable addition of loft so you can deliver the proper amount at impact.

This was the move that helped Walt stop popping it off the face and drastically improve his distance control.

Go

It's time to move. But you've got to be careful.

Your trail shoulder is the motor powering your putting stroke. Now, you might already know this. Unfortunately, someone probably taught you to create your putting motion by essentially rocking your shoulders, tilting the trail shoulder up on the backstroke, and letting it come back down on the forward stroke. That's what traditional putting instruction tells you to do, usually in an effort to help you master a straight-back-and-straight-through stroke. Not only is that the exact motion we're trying to avoid, but this shoulder-shrugging approach causes your upper body to tilt backward and your head to move. I can pretty much guarantee you've been told to keep your head still while putting, but that's tough to pull off when you're rocking your shoulders. It's darn near *impossible* if you've reached the age where those neck and shoulder muscles start to stiffen.

All this excess movement causes you to add loft at impact. This is killer for proper distance control and one of the key reasons golfers struggle on the greens.

What you want to do instead is let your trail shoulder rotate *back* on the backstroke instead of tilting upward.

To help my students conceptualize this, I often put my hand on their trail shoulder blade and have them push against my hand as they make their stroke. You can also find the feeling of this motion by standing upright with your arms crossed over your chest. Rotate your shoulders so your shoulder blades move backward and forward. That's the motion you're looking for to move the putter.

Once you've found that proper rotation in the trail shoulder for the backstroke, simply make the same motion from your new putting posture and set up.

It all sounds too basic to work, I know. But it does. Try it and see for yourself.

Then check out the next chapter for five putting drills that will help you make this lesson stick.

In Short...

The ALL-Go putting motion involves four basic phases:

1. **Aim** – Aim the line on the top of your putter in the direction you want the ball to start.
2. **Lock** – Grip the putter in your palm so the shaft aligns with your lead forearm.
3. **Load** – Tilt the shaft just enough so it loads into your lead forearm.
4. **Go** – Take your stroke, letting the trail shoulder work back and then down the line.

Chapter 4

Putting: The Practice

At the beginning of this section, I promised to help you clear out the clutter of golf tips and putting concepts that crowd your mind when you step onto the green. This chapter is where I make it happen.

This is where we turn the concepts you've learned into muscle memory. You don't have to work so hard to remember what to do when you've already built the habit into your body.

I'm about to share my five favorite putting drills of all time. I've used these drills countless times over three decades of coaching, and they're the best tricks I know for helping both amateur and professional golfers achieve the three putting objectives consistently.

These drills are going to make a *massive* difference in your game.

Drill #1: Lead Foot Only Drill

What It's Good For:

If you're constantly coming out of putts, pulling your head, or doing anything else that knocks you off center in your stance, the Lead Foot Only Drill will help.

Practice this one regularly, and you'll get much better at keeping your body quiet, steady, and centered when you're on the green.

Steps:

The Easy Break

1. Instead of taking your regular putting stance, position your lead foot in line with the golf ball.
2. Balance all your weight on the lead foot, resting the toe of your trail foot on the ground behind you for support. (You can lift the trail foot if you prefer, but I typically recommend using it as a kickstand for safety and stability.)
3. Hit some putts from this position.

Why It Works:

Because you're balancing on one foot, your body has no choice but to remain still and centered. Any temptation to move your head or stand up is overridden by your body's instinct to stay upright.

Run this drill often enough, and you'll get so used to the stillness that you maintain it even with both feet planted firmly on the ground.

Drill #2: Trail Hand Only Drill

What It's Good For:

You remember that one of our key objectives in putting is to maintain a proper pace. Or, to put it another way, we need distance control. And the key to distance control?

Touch and feel.

Every terrific putter has excellent touch and feel—a solid sense of the speed and cadence they need to bring to their stroke in order to get the ball to roll the correct distance. You see it when you watch the all-time greats. Even when they don't get the ball in the hole, it's always close, always in line with the cup. Maybe their aim wasn't perfect or they misread the green by a hair. But the distance? They had it down.

If touch and feel is an area of struggle for you, as it is for most amateur golfers, the Trail Hand Only Drill will be a game-changer.

Steps:

1. Get set up to the golf ball.
2. Hold the putter in your trail hand only.
3. Put your lead hand in your pocket.
4. Roll some putts.

Why It Works:

Your trail hand is your dominant hand. That means it's the hand that's best at judging, sensing,

The Easy Break

and reacting to things like mass, friction, slope, power, and speed.

It's the same reason you use your dominant hand to throw a softball or a football. The same reason you wouldn't count on your non-dominant hand to lead you to victory in a corn hole tournament.

When you take your lead hand out of the equation, it's easier to pick up on the information your trail hand is giving you. If the ball rolls too fast, you'll have a clearer sense of how much you need to back off. If it's too short, your dominant hand will know how much to speed it up.

Of course, you wouldn't want to putt this way in a round. But this drill does a great job of helping you tune into what your trail hand is telling you.

Drill #3: Pause and Go Drill

What It's Good For:

Just like with a full swing, one of the toughest parts of the putting motion is **the transition**.

The transition is that moment when the clubhead changes direction. You go from swinging back to swinging forward. It's a sudden shift that can disrupt your pace, tempo, and cadence. If you tend to decelerate or "pop" your putts, the transition is the culprit.

Fortunately, you're about to learn a drill that will help you fine-tune your transition without even thinking about it.

Steps:

Take a backstroke, then Pause at the end of the stroke. **Count one thousand one, one thousand two, and swing through.**

1. Take your regular putting setup.
2. Swing the putter back, then at the end of your backstroke, pause and count, "One thousand one, one thousand two."
3. After that two-second pause, go ahead and swing through.

Why It Works:

The Pause and Go Drill allows you to stop and notice what happens in that transition. For example, are you closing the clubface? Are you rushing the downstroke? Are you slowing the putter down?

When you can observe it, you can change it.

Drill #4: Dime Drill

What It's Good For:

The Dime Drill is one of my favorite drills for **improving aim**. Or, to put it in terms of your putting objectives, this is the drill that's going to help you work on delivering a square face at impact.

Steps:

*In addition to your putter and ball, you'll need **a Sharpie**, **alignment rod**, and **dime** (or anything similar in size, like a penny or ball marker).

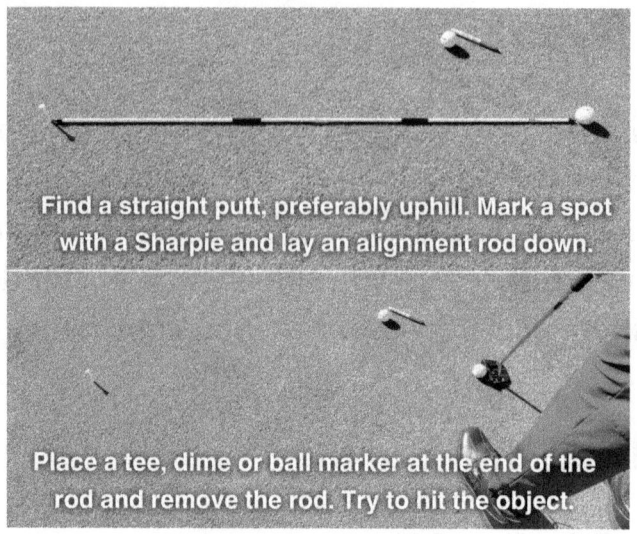

1. Find a putt that's going to be fairly straight; try to avoid a break if you can. I also recommend an uphill putt for this drill whenever possible.
2. Use your Sharpie to put a dot on the green in the spot where you plan to place your ball.
3. Lay the alignment rod on the ground in front of the dot, pointing directly uphill.
4. Place a dime or golf tee on the target end of the alignment rod.
5. Remove the rod.
6. Put your ball on the dot you drew.
7. Take a putt, trying to hit the dime or tee with the ball.

The Easy Break

Why It Works:

Because you're set up for a straight putt with no break—and because you're trying to hit a very specific point that's only about four feet away—you get a crystal clear picture of how the clubface is oriented at impact.

If you're a right-handed golfer and roll putts left of the dime, you know you're closing the face. If you roll putts to the right, you're opening it. And if you're nailing the dime, you're fulfilling that objective of delivering a square clubface.

It's hard to get that kind of clarity in a regular game. You'll almost always contend with some kind of slope, making it nearly impossible to tell if your putt veered left because you misread the green or because you closed your clubface. And the longer your putt is, the harder it becomes to judge your face control skills based on how your ball rolls.

The Dime Drill shows you exactly what you're doing so you can fix the right problem.

Drill #5: Box Drill

What It's Good For:

If you're struggling with **distance control on**

those long putts, this is the drill you're looking for.

The Box Drill helps you naturally discover the correct pace in your lag putting, and let me tell you, that is one of the skills that separates the all-time greats from the rest of us.

Steps:

1. Set up for a long putt—about 20-30 feet from the hole to start. As you get better at this drill, you can move farther back.
2. Position an alignment rod about 3-4 feet behind the cup. It should be perpendicular to the target line and centered behind the hole. This creates a

visual box: about 4 feet from one end of the alignment rod to the other and 4 feet from the front of the cup to the alignment rod.
3. Start putting. Your goal is to get the ball somewhere inside that box without hitting the alignment rod.

Why It Works:

When most amateur golfers practice long putts, they focus on the hole—this precision target 30 feet away. But lag putting isn't about draining it. If you do it, great! But the primary goal is to set yourself up for an easy second putt.

The Box Drill opens up your target. Now you're focused on an *area* instead of a single point, which allows you to worry less about making the putt and more about finding the right rhythm and pace to roll the ball the proper distance.

In Short...

Each of the five drills above can play a unique role in your putting practice. The next time you hit the practice green, zero in on the exercises that help with your specific areas of weakness.

Don't Forget!

You can find videos to support the instruction in this book at VLSGolf.com/EasyBreakTips or by scanning the QR code below.

Chapter 5

Putting: The Mistakes

Now that you know what a successful putting motion looks like, let's talk about the common mistakes that may have snuck into your stroke.

We'll go over three errors I see amateur golfers make all the time. You'll learn what these putting faults are, how to know if you're making them, and —most importantly—how to crush these bad habits and shave strokes off your score.

Let's get to it.

Mistake #1: Adding Loft at Impact

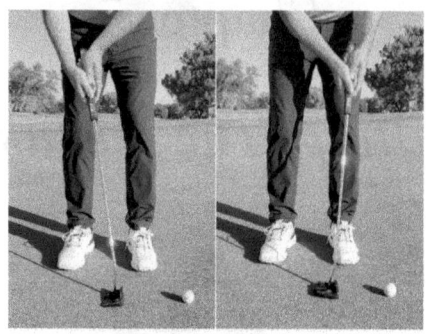

Mistake: Adding Loft   Correct: Maintaining Loft

You Might Be Making This Mistake If:

- You struggle with distance control.
- The ball hops when you hit it.

What's Happening:

As I mentioned in the chapter on objectives, a standard putter has about three degrees of loft built into the face. That's the ideal loft for getting the ball to roll the way you want it to on the green.

Unfortunately, casual golfers tend to hit the ball on a slightly upward angle and also tend to add loft. Now they're delivering six, seven, even eight degrees of loft at impact. This causes the ball to hop, destroying any hope of distance control or a decent roll.

The Easy Break

Nearly every amateur makes this mistake. It's probably the most common error I see on the green.

How to Get Past It:

The **Box Drill** will help. That's the distance control drill you learned in the last chapter. I'll share the steps again here so you don't have to flip back to that section.

1. Set up for a long putt—about 20-30 feet from the hole to start. As you get better at this drill, you can move farther back.
2. Position an alignment rod about 3-4 feet behind the cup. It should be perpendicular to the target line and centered behind the hole. This creates a visual box: about 4 feet from one end of the alignment rod to the other and 4 feet from the front of the cup to the alignment rod.
3. Start putting. Your goal is to get the ball somewhere inside that box without hitting the alignment rod.

You're not directly working with loft in this drill, but it's a fix your body might make naturally as you work to improve your distance control.

You'll also make this mistake less as you master the "Aim, Lock, Load, and Go" system. On "Load," you lean the butt end of the putter forward so it's equal to the front side of the golf ball. Keep this angle throughout your stroke, and you'll maintain the proper loft as you make contact with the ball. **This is key for controlling proper loft on the putter.**

The **Pause and Go Drill** can help you notice these habits. Here's a quick refresher on how that one works:

1. Take your regular putting setup.
2. Swing the putter back, then at the end of your backstroke, pause and count, "One thousand one, one thousand two."
3. After that two-second pause, go ahead and swing through.

Use the pause to notice if you're hinging your wrists and shifting the direction of the butt end of the club.

Mistake #2: Poor Face Control on Short Putts

You Might Be Making This Mistake If:

The Easy Break

- You struggle to sink short putts.
- You're consistently pushing or pulling your putts.

What's Happening:

The hole is *right there.* It seems like it should be so easy to keep the ball on a straight line for four measly feet.

But you and I both know it's not. Your putter only has to be a tiny bit closed to send the ball rolling too far left. That's why delivering a square clubface is everything.

How to Get Past It:

The **Dime Drill** you learned in the last chapter is fantastic for practicing face control. If you need a reminder, that's the drill that goes like this:

1. Find a putt that's going to be pretty straight; try to avoid a break if you can. I also recommend an uphill putt whenever possible.
2. Use your Sharpie to put a dot on the green in the place where you plan to put your ball.

3. Lay the alignment rod on the ground in front of the dot, pointing directly at your target.
4. Place a dime or tee on the target end of the alignment rod.
5. Remove the rod.
6. Put your ball on the dot you drew.
7. Take a putt, trying to hit the dime or tee with the ball.

If you want to take it a step further, I recommend the **Frontline Drill**. You'll need a **Sharpie** and **alignment rod** for this one, too. Here's how it works:

1. Find a putt that's going to be pretty straight.

2. Use the Sharpie to draw a dot on the green.
3. Place an alignment rod right on top of the dot, pointing at the center of the cup.
4. Roll the rod just enough to reveal the dot.
5. Draw a 3-4" line along the rod right in front of the dot.
6. Place the ball on the dot and practice a few putts, using the line on your putter and the line on the green to help you aim your putts.

This is the best way I know to practice precision face control. If your clubface is the slightest bit open or closed, you'll feel it. Then you'll fix it.

Mistake #3: Reading the Green Incorrectly

You Might Be Making This Mistake If:

- You feel good about your speed control and face control, but you're still not making putts.

What's Happening:

You underestimate a dip. You overestimate a hill. You aim for the front of the cup without realizing it's impossible to roll the ball straight in from its current position.

The green can feel like an optical illusion sometimes, and few things in this game are as frustrating as hitting a great putt that makes a wild left turn because of a slope you couldn't see. If you've got a bad habit of misreading the green, you'll have to address it to see better scores.

How to Get Past It:

I've got three green-reading tips that'll make it so much easier to see the contours of the carpet and visualize the roll of your ball.

First, always start by walking the path from the ball to the cup. Your feet can tell you so much more about the shape of the ground than your eyes will. So pay attention. Notice how the earth slopes under your feet. Feel how steep or shallow the breaks are.

Then return to the ball, look back at the hole, and ask yourself where the ball is going to enter the cup. For example, if you

The Easy Break

have to contend with a break sloping downward from right to left, you'll have to hit the ball well to the right of the cup so it will roll up onto the incline and drop into the hole from the right side. So you want to aim your putt with that goal in mind.

When you practice this visualization, you might even like to create a time-lapse for yourself like you see in the image below. Just use your Sharpie to put a dot on the green where your ball will go. Then, drop a few balls between that spot and the cup, representing different points you expect your ball to hit as it rolls over the slope of the green and into the hole.

Give yourself a moment to see that path, then remove the balls and roll a few putts, aiming to recreate that journey.

My last tip is to pick a target between you and the cup. As you visualize the path you expect your ball to take, find something along that track that can serve as a guide. It could be a pitch mark, a different color of grass, whatever. Take your putt with the goal of rolling the ball over that spot as it heads toward the cup.

In Short...

If you keep adding loft at impact:

- Practice the Box Drill.
- Remember to Load the handle of your putter so the butt end is equal to the front of the ball. Keep the butt end of the putter in front of the clubhead throughout your stroke.

If you're struggling with face control:

- Practice the Dime Drill.
- Practice the Frontline Drill.

If you're always misreading the green:

- Walk the path of your ball to feel the slope of the green in your feet.
- Visualize where the ball is going to enter the cup.

The Easy Break

- Pick a spot along the path you expect your ball to travel and try to roll the ball over that spot.

Chapter 6

Putting: The Situations

Now you've learned a new putting system that makes it easy to meet all three crucial objectives consistently. You've learned a ton of drills to help you master your new putting stroke, and you've put a little time in on the practice green, fixing the putt-sabotaging errors you didn't realize you were making.

You're excited to hit the course with your new skills. You and your golf partner walk up to the green on the first hole. You've got your putter in hand, ready to show off. Then you see that they've aerated the greens.

Little potholes everywhere.

That's the nature of the game, isn't it? You can

practice and perfect, but golf still finds a way to throw new challenges at you.

In this chapter, I'm going to give you a few strategies for all those little what-ifs. And I have a feeling you'll be surprised by how well you manage these unexpected situations the next time you encounter them.

Putts on the Fringe   Sandy Greens   Downhill Putts

Situation #1: On the Fringe

Your ball is on the fringe, right up against the collar. Technically your ball is not on the green, but in this situation, you will want to use your putter. Visually speaking, it's an intimidating situation. All that long grass is sure to interfere with your stroke. But when you know what to do, it's really not that bad.

You've got two options in this situation. **You**

The Easy Break

can use your putter *or* you can use a hybrid.

If you go with your putter, you'll want to change your setup. Our goal is to get good, clean contact, which means we have to get around the grass.

To do this, position the ball in the center of your stance. This puts it back slightly from where it is in your regular putting setup. That's because you want to make contact on a slight *descending* motion to avoid catching grass between the clubface and the ball.

Then add a tiny bit of loft. To do that, move your hands back slightly at address.

Now, I know I've just spent several pages telling you over and over again that adding loft is the last thing you want to do on the green, but in this case, that extra loft is going to put a little hop on the ball, and that's going to get it off the fringe.

If you'd rather solve this problem with a hybrid, grab the one with the least amount of loft and set up like you would with a putter under normal circumstances. No need to change your ball position or add loft. Then, roll the ball using a putting motion. Because of its rounded bottom and additional loft, the hybrid will glide right through the grass and send your ball rolling onto the green.

Situation #2: Aerated Greens

You might also refer to it as "plugged greens." Whatever you call it, it can send any golfer into a panic. How are you supposed to navigate that pockmarked terrain?

Once again, the secret is to add loft at address. **Take your normal putting setup, but move your hands back ever so slightly—about half an inch.** That little move changes your loft from about three degrees to five degrees. Believe it or not, that seemingly insignificant adjustment is all it takes to get the ball rolling on an aerated green.

Situation #3: Downhill Putts

Nothing makes a golfer sweat like a steep downhill putt. Those shots can get away from you fast. But I've got three little tricks that will give you a lot more confidence as you approach the slope in the future.

First, walk the path of your ball. Get a good feel for the incline with your feet so you can get a better sense of how fast that ball is going to roll.

Second, when you get set up, focus your eyes on the front edge of the cup.

That's what you're shooting for in terms of distance control.

Third, notice your grip pressure. You want lighter than average pressure in your grip for downhill putts.

That's it. Those three deceptively simple tricks are going to make managing the dreaded downhill putt much, much easier.

In Short...

When your ball lands on the fringe:

- Position the ball in the center of your stance.
- Add a tiny bit of loft at address.
- Consider using a hybrid.

For aerated greens:

- Add loft by moving your hands back about half an inch at address.

For downhill putts:

- Walk the path of your ball to get a feel for the slope with your feet.
- Focus your eyes on the front of the cup.

Todd Kolb

- Use a lighter grip pressure than you normally would.

Chapter 7

Putting: A Recap

My goal in working with students is to make this game less overwhelming, not more so. If your mind is reeling from all the new information you just took in, I recommend taking a step back to look at the big picture. This section will help you do exactly that.

Below, you'll find a quick recap of the things we covered in each chapter. Skim through it and see how all these parts work together to create one simple system. Make a note of any chapters you want to revisit. You can even download a PDF of this recap at www.VLSCoaching.com/BookOffer for quick reference the next time you're on the golf course or practice green.

Here's everything you just learned in a nutshell:

The Objectives

When you putt, focus on three key objectives:

1. Delivering a **square clubface**
2. Delivering the **proper loft**
3. Maintaining the **proper pace with your putter head**

Traditional approaches to the putting stroke make achieving these objectives more difficult than it has to be.

The easiest and most effective technique for amateur golfers is the ALL-Go putting system: **slight arc on the backstroke and straight down the line as you swing through.**

The Foundation

To nail your putting setup, do the following:

- Position your feet a standard putter grip's length (about 10 inches) from the ball.
- Use whatever stance width works for you—just be consistent.
- Position the ball slightly forward of center in your putting stance.

The Easy Break

- Align your lead eye with the inside (trail side) of the golf ball.
- Set up with 60-65% of your weight in your lead foot.
- Place the putter in the palm of your lead hand, then add your trail hand with the palm facing the target.

The Motion

The ALL-Go putting motion involves four basic phases:

1. **Aim** – Aim the line on the top of your putter in the direction you want the ball to start.
2. **Lock** – Hold the putter so the grip works through the lifeline of your lead hand.
3. **Load** – Move the butt end of the grip ever so slightly toward the target.
4. **Go** – Take your stroke, letting the trail shoulder work back and then down the line.

The Practice

To practice keeping your body steady and quiet in your putts, use the Lead Foot Only Drill:

1. Instead of taking your regular putting stance, position your lead foot in line with the golf ball.
2. Balance all your weight on the lead foot, resting the toe of your trail foot on the ground behind you for support. (You can lift the trail foot if you prefer, but I typically recommend using it as a kickstand for safety and stability.)
3. Roll some putts from this position.

To improve your touch and feel, use the Trail Hand Only Drill:

1. Get set up to the golf ball.
2. Hold the putter in your trail hand only.
3. Put your lead hand in your pocket.
4. Roll some putts.

To work on your transition, use the Pause and Go Drill:

The Easy Break

1. Take your regular putting setup.
2. Swing the putter back, then at the end of your backstroke, pause and count, "One thousand one, one thousand two."
3. After that two-second pause, go ahead and swing through.

To improve your aim, use the Dime Drill:

1. Find a putt that's going to be pretty straight; try to avoid a break if you can. I also recommend an uphill putt for this drill whenever possible.
2. Use your Sharpie to put a dot on the green in the place where you plan to put your ball.
3. Lay the alignment rod on the ground in front of the dot, pointing directly at your target.
4. Place a dime on the target end of the alignment rod.
5. Remove the rod.
6. Put your ball on the dot you drew.
7. Take a putt, trying to hit the dime with the ball.

To practice distance control, use the Box Drill:

1. Set up for a long putt—about 20-30 feet from the hole to start. As you get better at this drill, you can move farther back.
2. Position an alignment rod about 3-4 feet behind the cup. It should be perpendicular to the target line and centered behind the hole. This creates a visual box: about 4 feet from one end of the alignment rod to the other and 4 feet from the front of the cup to the alignment rod.
3. Start putting. Your goal is to get the ball somewhere inside that box without hitting the alignment rod.

The Mistakes

Overcome common putting mistakes with the practice strategies that follow.

If you keep adding loft at impact:

- Practice the Box Drill.
- Remember to Load the handle of your putter by moving the top of the grip slightly toward the target.

The Easy Break

- Keep the butt end of the putter in front of the clubhead throughout your stroke.

If you're struggling with face control:

- Practice the Dime Drill.
- Practice the Frontline Drill.

If you're always misreading the green:

- Walk the path of your ball to feel the slope of the green in your feet.
- Visualize where the ball is going to enter the cup.
- Pick a spot along the path you expect your ball to travel and try to roll the ball over that spot.

The Situations

Maintain control in hairy situations with the following fixes.

When your ball lands on the fringe:

- Position the ball in the center of your stance.

- Add a tiny bit of loft at address by moving your hands back sightly.
- Consider using a hybrid.

For aerated greens:

- Move your hands back about half an inch at address to add loft.

For downhill putts:

- Walk the path of your ball to get a feel for the slope.
- Focus your eyes on the front of the cup.
- Use a lighter grip pressure than you normally would.

Getting exciting? You should be. This new knowledge is going to completely transform your golf game. When you're ready to take it a step further, join me in the next section to talk chipping.

Notes

Use this space to write any notes of your own. What's your biggest takeaway? What skills or concepts do you want to prioritize in your putting practice?

Part Two

Chipping

Chipping is Emily's favorite skill. She sees it as a potential game-changer, and I can confirm it's been exactly that in many of her tournaments. As she explains it:

"I might miss the green, but then I'll chip it super close or even chip it in. Now I have a par or a birdie, and I thought I was going to bogey this hole. It's good momentum. I know I can clean it up around the green, get up and down when I need to. I think that's really given me a competitive edge because I don't think the other girls expect that."

That's the kind of power Barry tapped into when he had a *huge* chipping victory during a recent VLS Golf School. I'll let him tell the story.

"I got up and down from thirty yards on one hole. That's something that's never happened to me. It was a little pitch shot. I hit it up to three feet and made the putt. I was so excited when that happened. I didn't care about the rest of the round after that point."

That's the kind of win that'll make your whole day, especially considering how unpredictable chip shots can be. Or how unpredictable they can *seem*, anyway. As Claire explains it:

"They say your worst putt is better than your worst chip. You can putt the ball and get within the range of the hole, but with a chip, you can go off the toe and get in the sand or not have the distance control and go way beyond the hole. With chipping, consistency is the most difficult thing."

She's not wrong. From the position of the lie to the position of the hole, there are several relevant factors to consider when you approach any chip shot. The only strategy most golfers know is to hinge their wrists and see what happens. I'm glad to say you're about to learn a far more reliable method.

For Walt, consistency wasn't the issue. In fact, he was *consistently* chili dipping it.

"Even when I got it up on the green, it was way too short," he said. "Now I'm chipping a lot that go right up near the hole or within three feet, five feet. I would say 95% of the time, I'm around the hole.

The Easy Break

At the course where I live now, a lot of guys putt from off the green, and I feel more confident chipping. Of all my short-game shots, that's the area where I've improved the most."

So what changed for Walt?

You're about to find out. You'll learn all the tricks I taught him, plus the one revelation that made a huge impression on both him and Claire.

I'll also share the tip that was an absolute game-changer for Barry. I'm proud to say he actually learned that one from my son.

We've got a lot of fun stuff coming up, so let's get into it.

Chapter 8

Chipping: The Objectives

When you're this close to the green, it seems crazy to think about any goal other than getting the ball as close to the hole as possible.

But you know how this works by now. Before you can reach that goal, you have to focus on certain objectives within your swing. What needs to happen in your chip shot in order for you to get the ball where you want it to go?

Once again, we're looking at three key objectives.

The Three Objectives of Chipping

Objective One: You need a little bounce. You know how your wedge has some curve on the bottom of the clubhead? We call that bounce or roll, and it's the secret to getting the clubhead to move through the turf without digging, grabbing, or otherwise killing your chip shots.

While it's true that bounce is already built into your equipment, you still have the power to interrupt or enhance this feature with your swing motion. You'll learn more about that as we go along.

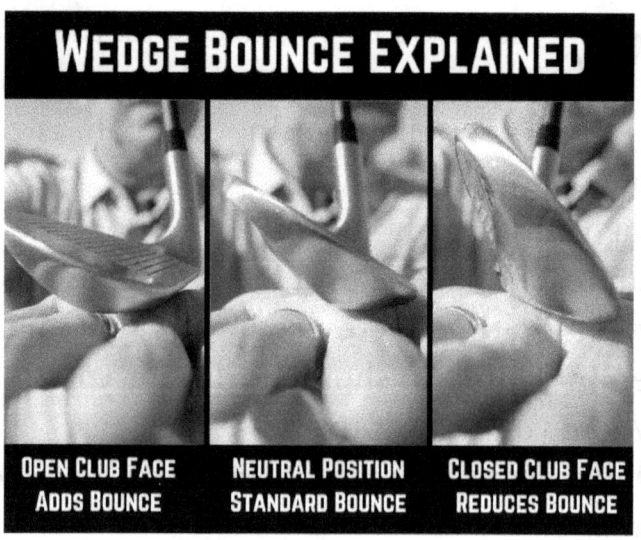

Objective Two: Make impact on a downward angle of attack. To put it another way, you want to make contact with the ball while the clubhead is still traveling at a downward angle before it hits the ground and starts moving upward again.

As you continue through this section, you'll often see me refer to the "low point" of your swing. The low point is the moment in your swing when the clubhead reaches the lowest point of the motion. In general, you want the low point of your swing *in front* of the golf ball when you're chipping. That way, the clubhead hits the ball while it's still traveling downward, before it reaches the low point.

Objective Three: Pick the right club for the shot. This is a crucial element of any successful chip shot... and you're probably making it way too complicated for yourself. You'll learn how to achieve Objectives One and Two as you read on, but let's lay the groundwork for Objective Three right now.

Club Selection for Chip Shots

Many golfers like to chip with several different clubs—7-iron, 8-iron, 9-iron, pitching wedge, sand wedge, you name it. And listen, I understand why. When you've got that many options on hand, it seems like you should be able to select the exact perfect tool for the job.

But that logic only plays out if you've got enough time to do a good amount of playing and even more practicing. Otherwise, you become a jack of all clubs, master of none. I mean, if you're pulling out your 9-iron to make a chip shot only about once or twice a round, how will you ever get good at chipping with that specific club?

My advice? **Pick two clubs.** Every time

you've got to make a chip shot, you can only make it with one of those two clubs. Block out your golf partner's voice when they're insisting that you'd do better with a third option. Forget the article you read about how a 7-iron is your best weapon in this specific chipping scenario. Just narrow your focus to your *two* designated chipping clubs and pick the one that will perform best in the current situation.

There will be times when you're tempted to widen your options. But trust me on this. You'll gradually get so comfortable with those two clubs you'll have more success with them in *every* scenario, even when traditional wisdom says you'd be crazy not to use one of the clubs you've excluded from consideration.

I personally use a 48° wedge and a 56° wedge. I use the 48° when I want the ball to roll a good distance after it lands on the green. When I want more fly and less roll, I opt for a 56° club.

It's up to you what your go-to clubs will be, but the basic rule of thumb is this:

- **Lower loft** for **less fly** and **more roll**
- **Higher loft** for **more fly** and **less roll**

In Short...

- In every chip shot, you want to meet three objectives: use the bounce of the club, make contact at a downward angle, and choose the right club for the job.
- Instead of giving yourself several clubs to choose from, select *two* that will be your go-to clubs for chip shots. That will ensure you have more opportunities to practice and master them in a range of chipping situations.
- Use your lower lofted wedge when you want less ball flight and more roll. Use a higher lofted club when you're looking for a higher ball flight and less roll.

Chapter 9

Chipping: The Foundation

Now that we know what we're trying to pull off in our chip shots, it's time to lay the groundwork to make it happen. In other words, we gotta talk setup.

Everything you're about to learn is designed to help you achieve those first two objectives: taking full advantage of your clubhead's built-in bounce and making impact on a downward angle.

Follow all these setup tips and you'll be able to accomplish those goals without even thinking about it. And if it all starts to feel like a little too much to digest, don't worry. What sounds complicated in words is actually pretty simple in practice, which is why I've ended this chapter with a visual summary for clarity.

Feet Position

For chip shots, we typically want the feet closer together than they would be for a full swing or putting stroke. **I generally recommend getting your toes about hip-width apart**, but if you feel unbalanced in this position, feel free to widen your stance a little.

You also want your heels closer together than your toes. In other words, **we're looking for a slight outward flare of the toes, roughly 20° or so.** This slight toe flare will help with your balance and stability, which are key to good chipping.

Distance From the Ball

One of the most common chipping errors I see among amateurs is that they stand too far from the ball. You don't want this to look like the setup for a regular full swing. You want to get in there nice and snug—almost uncomfortably close.

As a checkpoint, **try to feel like your chin is almost over the golf ball—maybe just a couple inches short of the ball.** It'll feel a little weird at first, but you'll get used to it in time. More importantly, you'll see results. This close position makes it easier to get the club shaft at an optimal angle. That brings us to...

Shaft Position

Once you're in position, **raise the club shaft slightly so it moves toward the golf ball.** You're looking for a more upright angle here. This sets you up nicely for the proper swing motion. You'll see what I mean in the next chapter.

You also want a *very* slight forward lean on the shaft to help achieve that all-important downward strike. **Think about aligning the butt end of the club with the front side of the golf ball. Don't go beyond that point.** A lot of golfers lean the shaft too far forward. That error comes with disastrous results, as you'll learn in the Mistakes chapter.

Weight in Feet

If you've read *The Bad Lie*, you know I love that 60/40 split: 60% of your body weight in the lead foot, 40% in the trail foot at setup.

For chip shots, however, 60% is the *minimum* for the lead foot. **It's better to get about 65-70% of your weight forward.** Not that you have to worry about exact measurements. You don't have to run out and get a pressure mat or smart insoles. The bottom line is that you want to feel just a bit more pressure in that lead foot at setup than you would for the regular VLS golf swing.

You're also going to *keep* most of that pressure in the lead foot throughout your swing. There's very little weight shift. The whole point is to stabilize the body because excess body movement is one of the biggest reasons amateur golfers struggle with chipping.

Clubface Aim

As you position your golf club, open the clubface slightly. *Very* slightly. **We're shooting for**

around 3-4° open. This will add bounce and loft, both of which are essential for a solid chip shot.

Ball Position

This might be the most important part of the entire setup. See, your ball position largely determines the angle at which the club will come in contact with the ball. Position the ball too far forward, and you'll catch it *after* the low point of your swing when the clubhead is moving at an upward angle. Get it too far back in your stance, and the club will be moving at a sharp descending angle, and you won't make solid, centered contact.

A lot of golfers get the ball too far back. **You want it to be in the dead center of your stance—in the middle of your heels.**

Use an alignment rod or another club to find the perfect ball position. Simply lay the rod or club on the ground so it tracks straight out from the golf ball, toward your feet. Then take your stance with the rod right in the middle of your heels. Now you've got the ball dead center, and you're ready to start making some chip shots.

In Short...

- Stand with your toes about hip-width apart, heels close together for a slight toe flare.
- Stand close enough to the ball that your chin is just a couple inches from hovering directly over the ball.

The Easy Break

- Lean the club shaft toward the ball just slightly and toward the target so that the butt end of the club aligns with the front side of the golf ball.
- Get about 65-70% of your body weight in your lead foot.
- Open the clubface a little.
- Position the golf ball in the center of your stance.

Chapter 10

Chipping: The Motion

I hope you're up for a little dancing. That's basically what good chipping looks like... what it *is*. Watch any legendary golfer take a chip shot, and you'll see it: the natural, rhythmic way they move with the club. It's like watching ballet.

When you've got a driver in your hands, you're all about speed and force. With a putter, you're thinking about touch and feel—about precision and control.

Chipping lands somewhere in the middle. You're not smoking it. You're not fine-tuning it. You're just following the motion.

You know, dancing.

Of course, you can't learn a new technique through metaphors alone. So, let's go over the components your chipping motion needs to have in order to accomplish that sense of steady, coordinated motion and fulfill the objects we laid out two chapters ago.

I'm going to walk you through five key checkpoints that make up a successful chipping motion, starting with the takeaway.

The Butt End of the Club on the Takeaway

As you swing back from the golf ball, make sure the butt end of the club is moving away from the target.

I know—*where else would it go*, right? But take a chip shot using your current technique and pay attention to what the butt of your club actually does. You might see the answer.

A lot of amateur golfers hinge their wrists when they're chipping. The clubhead might be moving away, but the butt of the club is tilting toward the target.

The Easy Break

You want to kill the hinge. That one change makes a massive difference in your chipping, and you'll see why as we go along.

In fact, if you only remember one thing from this chapter, let this be it. Make sure the butt of the club initially moves away from the target, just like the clubhead does.

Face Orientation

Another tip for the takeaway: rotate the toe of your club open just a little as it moves back. This is going to add loft and bounce.

Now, you might be wondering why you're

opening the clubface again after you already opened it slightly in your setup. The idea is to counteract a bad habit nearly every amateur golfer has. Having worked with thousands of golfers, I *know* that the vast majority of them have a tendency to close the clubface on the takeaway when they're chipping. That error delofts the club and ruins the shot.

That's why you want to feel the clubface rotate open very slightly as you swing back. It's the most effective way to overcome that face-closing tendency and preserve the loft and bounce you need for a successful chip shot.

The Path of the Clubhead

Throughout your chipping motion, you want to make sure the clubhead stays out in front instead of working inside. Here's a trick for visualizing and practicing this concept:

Put an alignment rod or golf club on the ground halfway between your toes and the ball, parallel to the target line.

As you practice your swing, make sure the clubhead stays out in front of the rod during the entire motion. Or, to put it another way, keep the clubhead on the ball side of the alignment rod while your hands stay on the inside of the alignment rod. This clubhead-to-hands relationship is key for good, solid contact.

Body Weight

This is where the dancing comes in. Wherever your club goes, you're going with it.

In the Foundation chapter, we established that you want to set up with about 65-70% of your weight on your lead foot. **As you swing back, let a tiny bit of your weight shift into the trail foot, then move it back to the lead foot when you swing through.** This is not a full pivot like we see in the full swing but a slight movement *with* the club to create rhythm, touch, and feel.

You'll want to finish with a lot of your weight on the lead feet—I'm talking about 75-80%. As a good checkpoint, your trail heel should be just slightly off the ground; that'll help ensure you've got your weight forward.

The Butt End of the Club at the Finish

The last thing I want you to notice is where the butt end of the club is pointing when you finish your swing motion. You're checking for that nasty hinge habit again.

At the finish, the butt of the club should be pointing at your belt buckle or slightly in front of your belt buckle. If it's pointing all the way past your trail hip or beyond your lead hip, you've made a grave error that you'll definitely see reflected in your ball flight.

The Easy Break

Now, if you're thinking you've seen plenty of wrist hinge on the PGA Tour, you're not wrong. But I'll let Barry break this down.

"You see these guys on TV—you know, they've only chipped a *million* golf balls—and they're all loose, and they've got this nice flowing little move. But unless you've got 10,000 hours to spend practicing, you want to make it as simple as possible."

Bingo. Flipping the hands only works if you have time to train pro-level precision. Most casual golfers don't, which was why Barry kept hitting 'em fat. It wasn't until my son, JT, introduced him to the VLS chipping setup and got him to cancel the hinge habit that he saw real improvement. Or, in his words, "almost instant success."

That's a fair way to describe it, considering this was the same weekend Barry had that huge chipping victory I told you about at the beginning of this section.

I'm not kidding when I say some of the simplest adjustments have the biggest impact.

In Short...

Here's a quick checklist for a successful chipping motion:

- Get the butt end of the club moving away from the target on the takeaway.
- Rotate the toe open slightly as you swing back.
- Keep the clubhead traveling out in front throughout your swing instead of coming inside and wrapping around your body.
- Let your weight shift with the motion of the club. Start with 65-70% of your weight on the lead foot, shift it to the trail foot ever so slightly on the backswing, and bring it back to the lead foot as you swing through. Finish with most of your weight on the lead foot and your trail heel slightly off the ground.

The Easy Break

- At the finish, make sure the butt end of the club is pointing at your belt buckle or slightly in front of it.

Chapter 11

Chipping: The Practice

You know what comes next. We need to bridge the gap between your *knowledge* of the ideal chipping motion and what your body actually *does* after you set up to the ball.

In other words, we need to practice.

I'm going to teach you five drills that will make a world of difference in your chipping technique. All these exercises help you perfect your strategy by exaggerating the feel you're looking for... both the feel of the proper motion *and* the feel of common errors.

Let's start with a drill you already know and hopefully love.

Drill #1: Lead Foot Only Drill

What It's Good For:

If you're reading through the sections of this book in order, you already learned the Lead Foot Only drill as part of your putting practice. In that context, the goal was to stabilize the upper body.

It holds the same purpose in your chipping practice. More specifically, **this drill will help you avoid tilting your upper body away from the target as you swing through.** That move is murder, but so many amateur golfers do it.

Remember how we said you want to finish your swing with most of your weight on the lead foot? When you tilt away from the target, you do the opposite of that. You move your weight to the trail foot, which moves the low point of your swing farther back in your stance. As a result, you reach the low point *before* making contact with the golf ball. And you know what that means.

You're going to hit the ball with an *ascending* angle of attack, not the descending angle you want. You'll probably also chili dip it or scull it across the green.

Long story short, the Lead Foot Only Drill

helps you achieve the objective of making contact at a downward angle.

Steps:

1. Instead of taking your regular chipping stance, position your lead foot in line with the golf ball.
2. Balance all your weight on the lead foot, resting the toe of your trail foot on the ground behind you for support. (You can lift the trail foot if you prefer, but I typically recommend using it as a kickstand for the sake of safety and stability.)
3. Hit some chip shots from this position.

Why It Works:

This drill forces you to stabilize the upper body immediately. After all, if you tilt away, you'll lose your balance. Run the Lead Foot Only Drill regularly, and that upper body stillness will become second nature.

I also love this drill because it makes my students *aware*. Leaning away from the target is one of those habits that arises without thought or intention. It can be hard to notice you're even doing it.

When you're balanced on one foot, however, you feel it. That awareness is going to stay with you as you play a round of golf. If you start to tilt, you'll notice.

Drill #2: Trail Hand Only Drill

What It's Good For:

This is another one you'll recognize from the putting section. And just like with putting, the Trail Hand Only Drill is excellent for **improving touch and feel with your chip shots**.

Remember how I said that a great chipping motion is all about dancing with the club? This drill helps you find that movement—that rhythm and flow.

The Easy Break

In fact, to make sure you have a minute to find your tempo, let's add a few practice swings to this drill.

Steps:

1. Get set up without a golf ball.
2. Hold the club in your trail hand only.
3. Put your lead hand in your pocket.
4. Make a few continuous swing motions back and through.
5. Take a moment to get into the feel of it. Notice the rhythm of the club and your weight moving together back and through, back and through, back and through.

6. Step up to the ball and hit some chip shots.

Why It Works:

This drill may be a little frustrating at first. It's not easy to hit chip shots one-handed. But stick with it because once you get the hang of it, you'll start getting some valuable information from your trail hand.

See, your trail hand is also your dominant hand. It's more sensitive to nuanced sensations and movements like rhythm and tempo. When you take your lead hand out of the equation, it becomes easier to feel and respond with your dominant hand.

Drill #3: Lead, Trail, Middle Drill

What It's Good For:

Remember the final tip of the last chapter? The one about making sure the butt end of your club is pointed at your belt buckle or slightly in front of the buckle when you finish your swing?

That checkpoint basically tells you if you released the clubhead properly through impact. And that's important because the release is key for getting enough bounce and controlling where the clubhead hits the ground.

This drill helps you nail that belt buckle checkpoint every time by allowing you to feel the difference between getting it right and getting it wrong. Bonus: you'll also get to see how your release pattern influences the outcome of your swing.

In this exercise, you'll experiment with three different release patterns: lead pocket, trail pocket, and neutral (that's your belt buckle). You'll see what I mean when you read through the steps.

Steps:

1. Take your regular chipping setup.
2. Take a chip shot and finish with the butt end of the club pointing at your **lead pocket**.
3. Take another chip shot, this time finishing with the butt of the club pointing at your **trail pocket**.
4. Take another chip shot, finishing with the butt of the club pointing at your **belt buckle**.
5. Notice how each shot feels in your body and how the ball reacts.

Why It Works:

One of the best ways to find neutral is to experience the extremes. When your body knows what a lead pocket and trail pocket release feel like, it'll have a better sense of where neutral is.

This drill also shows you why that neutral release is so important. It shows you what happens—both in your body and to the ball—when your release is off. You'll likely notice that the ball is hot off the face and rolls a lot in the lead pocket release. A trail pocket release will have significantly more height and you'll feel your weight shifting back into your trail foot on the finish. Nothing helps a golfer course-correct faster than revealing how their habits create the exact shots they *don't* want.

Drill #4: Radius Control Drill

What It's Good For:

Ready to move on to some advanced studies? This drill will get you thinking about an aspect of your chip shots I bet no one has ever brought to your attention before. But man, does it matter.

This is the lesson that helped Walt stop chili dipping. It's how Claire found that consistency she was looking for. I can't wait to hear how it helps you.

In this drill, we're talking about the radius of your chipping motion—the distance between the butt end of your club and your belt buckle.

So, just as an example, let's say you've got about 8 inches between your belt buckle and the butt end of your club. There are three things that can happen with that radius as you make your chipping motion:

1. You maintain 8 inches of distance through the entire swing. That's the ideal outcome.
2. You widen the radius on your backswing and again as you swing through.
3. You narrow the radius on your backswing and again as you swing through.

Casual golfers have trouble maintaining a consistent radius in their chipping motion. And let me tell you, poor radius control is a *really* effective way to inadvertently move the low point of your swing and wreck your contact. **If you chunk a lot of**

The Easy Break

chip shots, this drill could be a game-changer.

It's a tricky one, though, so I recommend doing it without a ball.

Steps:

1. Take your regular chipping setup minus the golf ball.
2. Make your chipping motion, deliberately narrowing your radius as you swing back and through. For example, if you start with 8 inches, you'd narrow it to 4 inches on the backswing, come back to 8 as you pass

through the middle, and narrow it again to 4 as you finish.
3. Make another chipping motion, this time widening your radius on the backswing and follow through. You might go from 8 inches to 12 inches, for example.
4. Swing again, this time being careful to maintain the same radius throughout your swing.

*Please note that the measurements I use as examples are intended to help you visualize the kind of variance I'm talking about. Don't worry about the exact distance between your body and club.

Why It Works:

Just like with the previous drill, the goal is to work with the extremes so your body can find the middle. And once again, this exercise also helps you experience the effect of widening or narrowing your radius. When you widen your radius and feel your club dig into the ground, sending angry vibrations up through the shaft and into your arms, you'll be motivated to not make that mistake again.

I get chills just thinking about it.

Drill #5: Low Tee Drill

What It's Good For:

This drill is a lot of fun; there's not much thinking or calculating involved in this one. It's just a matter of noticing an outcome and letting your body find the fix.

The Low Tee Drill is all about learning to control where the club hits the ground. **It's another good one for any golfer who has trouble making clean, solid contact at the proper angle.**

You need a tee for this one.

Steps:

1. Tee up the golf ball, but tee it really low. You want it just on top of the ground.
2. Take a chip shot, trying to bump the tee ever so slightly forward.
3. If the tee completely breaks, you are hitting too down. If the tee does not move at all, you are not hitting down enough. If the tee breaks or shifts, tee it back up and try again.

Why It Works:

This is another one of those great drills where you can actually see what's happening when your technique isn't quite right. Plus, the simplicity of it makes it really fun to do and repeat. You're just taking chip shots until you can consistently hit the ball while bumping the tee slightly forward.

Simple concept. Fun goal. Big gains for your golf game.

In Short...

These five drills pretty much cover the amateur golfer's most likely areas of struggle. Start with the ones that touch on your greatest areas of weakness and practice all of them to see swift improvement in your chip shots.

Chapter 12

Chipping: The Mistakes

Mistakes happen. It's just the reality of the game. Even when we know exactly what we're *supposed* to do, we can still find ourselves tripping over the same old errors.

In this section, I want to help you solidify your chipping technique by tackling the three most common problem shots among amateur golfers. These swing faults can start to make you cringe whenever it's time to reach for that wedge again. They're heartbreaking errors. Greenside disasters. Scorecard busters.

But they're also completely fixable. In fact, you may be surprised how quickly you can turn these problems around.

Mistake #1: Poor Distance Control

You Might Be Making This Mistake If:

- You're consistently chipping it too long or too short.
- You don't feel like you have control over your flight-to-roll ratio.

What's Happening:

No matter what you do, you can't seem to get the ball to roll the right distance. The knee-jerk reaction is to assume it's a power issue—that you're either hitting it too hard or too soft. But most likely, the problem is coming from one of these five errors:

Possibility #1: You're hinging the butt end of the club toward the target on the takeaway. As we discussed, that's going to make the ball come out low and hot. You've officially lost control.

Possibility #2: You've got the ball too far back in your stance. That will cause you to make impact too far behind the low point of your swing at an extreme downward angle. This effectively delofts your club, which causes the ball to come out hot and low.

**Possibility #3: You're executing a trail

or lead pocket release. Remember the Lead, Trail, Middle Drill from the last chapter? You learned that you want to finish your swing with the butt end of the club pointing at or slightly in front of your belt buckle. If it's pointing toward your lead pocket, the ball's going to be hot off the face with a lot of roll. If the butt of your club is pointing toward your trail pocket at the finish, you're going to get a lot of height and not enough distance.

Possibility #4: Your touch and feel is off. That happens sometimes. Your technique is solid, but you're misjudging the pace you need to get the ball where you want it to go.

Possibility #5: You picked the wrong club. I've encouraged you to only give yourself two clubs to choose from, but even within that limited selection, it's possible to choose the wrong one.

How to Get Past It:

You're probably way ahead of me on this one. After all, you've already learned how to fix all the errors I just described.

But in the interest of being crystal clear, I'll lay all this out, anyway.

First, keep the butt end of the club moving away from the target on your takeaway.

Second, make sure the golf ball is in the center of your stance. That'll ensure you make impact at the right angle and deliver the correct amount of loft.

Third, take care to get the butt end of the club pointing at or slightly in front of your belt buckle in your post-impact position. If you do that, you'll have maintained the proper loft, which gives you much more control over your ball's trajectory.

Fourth, improve your touch and feel by using the Trail Hand Only Drill. Here it is again so you don't have to flip back to the previous chapter:

1. Get set up without a golf ball.
2. Hold the club in your trail hand only.
3. Put your lead hand in your pocket.
4. Make a few continuous swing motions back and through.
5. Take a moment to get into the feel of it. Notice the rhythm of the club and your weight moving together back and through, back and through, back and through.
6. Step up to the ball and hit some chip shots.

Fifth, choose your club based on how far you want the ball to fly versus roll. If you want it to roll farther than it flies, use your less lofted club. If you want a longer flight and less roll, use the club with the higher loft.

Mistake #2: Lousy Contact

You Might Be Making This Mistake If:

- You keep chunking it.
- You keep skulling it.
- You've started asking your golf partners to avert their eyes every time you have to make a chip shot.

What's Happening:

You're hitting behind the ball, making impact at the wrong angle, and finding it nearly impossible to get clean, centered contact. There are three likely explanations for this.

Possibility #1: Your body is rotating backward in the downswing. This is one of those habits that's easy to pick up without realizing it, and it's a guaranteed contact-killer. Any movement in the upper body is going to move the low point of your golf swing. In this case, backward rotation moves the low point farther back, causing you to hit behind the ball.

Possibility #2: You're bringing the club inside on the takeaway. Remember how we laid an alignment rod on the ground halfway between your feet and the ball to make sure you kept your clubhead out in front? If you're veering toward the inside on the takeaway, you'll likely hit behind the ball when you swing through.

**Possibility #3: You're closing the club-

face on the takeaway. I see golfers make this mistake all the time. Shutting the face will cause it to dig at the low point of your swing, canceling out the built-in bounce and causing the kind of chunk shot that reverberates all the way up through the club shaft.

How to Get Past It:

First, work on quieting your upper body if you notice yourself rotating backward in the downswing. Use the Lead Foot Only Drill. As you may recall, it works like this:

1. Instead of taking your regular chipping stance, position your lead foot in line with the golf ball.
2. Balance all your weight on the lead foot, resting the toe of your trail foot on the ground behind you for support. (You can lift the trail foot if you prefer, but I typically recommend using it as a kickstand for safety and stability.)
3. Hit some chip shots from this position.

Second, make sure you're keeping the clubhead outside as you swing back. Bring back the alignment rod if you're having trouble visualizing this. Lay it on the ground halfway between your toe line and the ball, parallel to the target line. Make sure the clubhead stays out in front of the alignment rod throughout your entire swing motion.

Third, rotate the toe of your clubface slightly open on the takeaway. This will prevent digging and make it easier to take advantage of your club's built-in bounce.

Mistake #3: Shanks

You Might Be Making This Mistake If:

- You're hitting it so far back on the heel or hosel that the ball travels low and sharply sideways.
- You sometimes think you might hate this game.

What's Happening:

I hate to even bring this up. Just typing the word sends a chill up my spine. But the shank shot happens, and we have to acknowledge it to fix it.

If you're regularly hitting the ball on the heel or hosel, the cause is likely one of three things.

The Easy Break

Possibility #1: You've got the shaft too low or have too much forward shaft lean at address. The lower the shaft, the more the club wants to swing around your body in the backswing, exposing the heel. Excessive forward shaft lean causes the hosel to work toward the golf ball. Either way, you're looking at impending disaster.

Possibility #2: The clubhead works too far in and around on the backswing, exposing the heel. As we just discussed, a low shaft angle can cause this to happen, but it can also be the consequence of an improper swing motion.

Possibility #3: You've got a lead pocket finish. Remember your release patterns. If you finish your chip shot with the butt end of your club pointing at your lead pocket, that's a strong indication that you've exposed the heel through the impact zone.

How to Get Past It:

The good news is that the issues that are most likely to cause your shanking problem are pretty easy to fix.

First, check your shaft angle at setup. Remember, when you're chipping, you want to stand close to the ball, similar to your putting setup. This alone will help you get a more upright angle on the club shaft. Then, once you're in position, raise the handle just a little bit more, shifting it slightly closer to the golf ball. After you've fixed the low shaft issue, make sure the shaft is only leaning toward the target enough for the handle to align with the target side of the ball. You want *some* forward shaft lean, but it should be very slight.

Second, make sure the clubhead works to the outside for your entire swing. If it helps, bring out the alignment rod again. Set it on the ground halfway between your toes and the ball, running parallel to the target line. Practice your chipping, watching to see that the clubhead always stays on the ball side of the alignment rod.

Third, always finish with the butt end

The Easy Break

of your club pointing at your belt buckle or slightly in front of your belt buckle.

Take the time to master these three fixes, and I guarantee you'll make those shanks a distant memory.

In Short...

If you're struggling with distance control:

- Keep the butt end of the club moving away from the target on the takeaway.
- Check to make sure you've got the golf ball in the center of your stance.
- Finish with the butt end of your club pointing at or slightly in front of your belt buckle.
- Work on touch and feel by practicing the Trail Hand Only Drill.
- Think twice about club selection. Use the less lofted club for more roll and a shorter flight. Use the higher lofted club for less roll and more flight.

If you're having serious contact issues:

- Make sure your upper body isn't rotating backward in the downswing. If it is, practice the Lead Foot Only Drill to kick the habit.
- Keep the clubhead to the outside throughout your swing. Place an alignment rod between your toes and the ball as a guide.
- Rotate the toe of your clubface slightly open on the takeaway.

If you can't stop shanking it...

- Make sure you set up closer to the ball than you would for other shots. Lift the handle a bit so the shaft is even more upright, and only allow for a slight forward shaft lean.
- Keep the clubhead working outside throughout your swing motion. Use an alignment rod as a guide if it helps.
- Finish with the butt end of your club pointing at or slightly in front of your belt buckle.

Chapter 13

Chipping: The Situations

So what do we do when this game throws us a less-than-ideal chipping situation? When we have to deal with sloped lies or deep rough? If you're like the average amateur golfer, your current strategy is probably to make your best effort and hope you can at least get through this round with your pride intact.

But I think you and I can shoot higher, so to speak. We're going to cover some of the trickiest chipping situations you're likely to encounter in a round of golf. I'll give you some quick and simple tips for handling them, and the next time you gotta hit it off hardpan, you'll know exactly what to do. You might even be giving your golf partner some pointers.

Situation #1: Downhill Lie

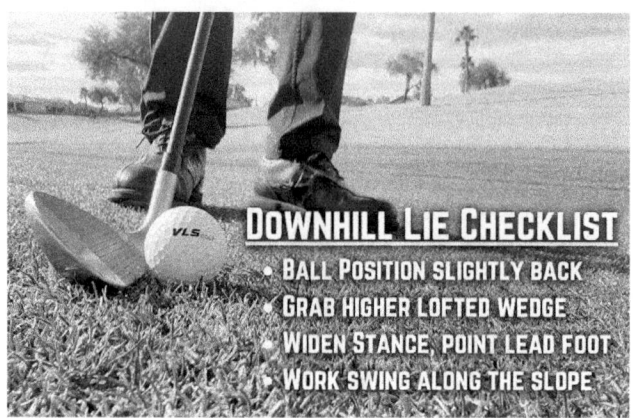

You've got the ball sitting on a downhill slope, the green's running away from you... how the heck are you supposed to make decent contact, let alone control your shot?

Let's put this together piece by piece.

Club Selection:

Grab your higher-lofted club. A downhill lie basically delofts your club, so you want to counter that as much as you can.

Setup:

Move the ball back slightly in your stance so it's just off the trail heel.

The Easy Break

Then **set up close to the ball and get that shaft a little more vertical.** It'll help you soften the shot.

On severe slopes, you can widen your stance slightly and point your lead foot down the slope. This will improve your overall balance as you move the club down the slope line.

Motion:

DOWNHILL LIE: CLUB WORKS DOWN SLOPE LINE

In the takeaway, make sure the butt of the club moves away from the golf ball like you would for any chip shot, but **make it feel almost like a putting motion**. Once again, this is going to soften the shot.

If you've got a severe slope, soften the shot even more by allowing the clubhead to work down the slope line as it goes through the impact zone.

Situation #2: Uphill Lie

You're looking at an opposite issue on an uphill lie. All things being equal, your ball is going to come out higher and softer from this position. Here's how you can manage the situation to stay in control of the trajectory.

Club selection:

Hitting it off an uphill slope will add loft, so pick your **less lofted club**.

The Easy Break

Setup:

Keep your setup the same as you would for any other chip shot, with one exception:

Move the ball back a little so it's off the inside of your trail heel. The uphill slope will push your body backward in your swing motion. As you know, that's going to move your low point back. Moving the ball back at setup ensures you'll still catch it on a downward motion.

Motion:

Your swing motion will be pretty much the same. Just be aware that if the green itself is uphill, that slope will soften the shot. It won't roll out as much as it would in other situations.

Now, a couple errors tend to pop up when we're working with an uphill lie—bad habits we might have eradicated from regular chip shots but find ourselves doing again when we're on an uphill slope.

Keep an eye on your weight distribution. Remember, your upper body will want to work toward the trail foot due to the slope. **So when you get set up, make sure you lean into that hill and stay there throughout the swing.**

The other thing you want to look out for is a change in your radius. As always, the goal is to **maintain a consistent radius** throughout your swing and **finish your chip shot with the butt end of your club pointing at your belt buckle.**

On an uphill lie, it's really easy to let the club get away from you, widening that radius and digging the clubhead into the ground.

Situation #3: Hardpan

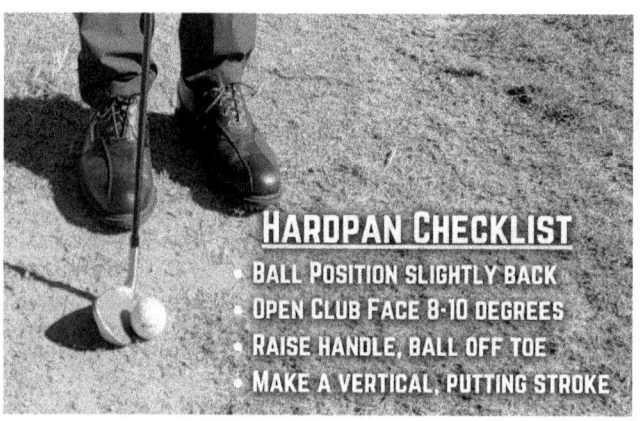

There will be times when your ball comes to rest on hardpan—an area where there's no grass. Or maybe the grass is just really soggy. Whatever the case may be, there's not a lot of turf under the ball. Soft or hard, we're going to handle it the same way.

The Easy Break

Club selection:

For this situation, you'll want your **less lofted club**.

Setup:

Once again, you're going to **move the ball back in your stance so it's in line with the inside of your trail heel.**

Then, rotate the clubface open a little more than usual. **If you're opening the clubface about 3-4° for regular chip shots, nudge it to about 8-10° for this one.** That's going to help the club move along the ground more easily.

Next, **lift the handle a bit so the club almost feels vertical with the ball positioned more off the toe of the clubface rather than the center.** The vertical shaft will help the clubhead work more like a putt, making the low point or contact point easier to control on this type of surface.

Motion:

For this chip shot, **you actually want to use a putting motion.** I even use a putting grip when I'm hitting it off hardpan.

A putting motion stays pretty level with the ground, and that will give you more forgiveness and a wider margin for error.

Situation #4: Deep Grass

Now, what about the opposite of hardpan? What do you do when your ball comes to rest in the deep grass? **The key formula here is a little extra speed combined with a lot of loft.** Those two elements working together will help you get the club through the turf and get the ball high in the air.

Let's talk about how you can make that happen.

Club selection:

Definitely reach for your **more lofted club**

on this one. That'll help you put more speed on it and get the ball up a little higher.

Setup:

Take a wide stance with even more toe flare. You'll need that stability to stay solid as you move the clubhead through the grass.

Yet again, you're going to **move the ball slightly back in your stance**.

Bend your knees so you feel like you're sitting nice and low. This physical position makes it easier for you to create a longer swing with more stability.

Finally, **rotate the clubface open a little more—about 8-10°**—to add some loft.

Motion:

To get out of the tall grass, **focus on creating a nice, long swing with some speed**. But now here's the kicker:

You're also going to go with a trail pocket release on this one.

You've seen the phrase "finish with the butt of the club pointing at your belt buckle" so many times in this book, I wouldn't be surprised if you were repeating it in your sleep at this point. But on this rare occasion, I want you to finish your chip shot with the butt of your club pointing toward the trail pocket.

When you make your swing with that goal in mind, you create a release that adds a little extra loft to your shot, helping you hoist the golf ball up over the tall grass.

In Short...

For a downhill lie:

- Use your highest lofted club.
- Move the ball back in your stance so it's just off the trail heel.
- Get closer to the ball and raise the shaft to a more vertical position.
- Make sure the butt end of the club moves away from the ball on the takeaway.
- Maintain a more level, almost putt-like motion.
- In the case of a severe slope, allow the clubhead to move down the slope line as it travels through the impact zone.

The Easy Break

For an uphill lie:

- Use your less lofted club.
- Move the ball back in your stance so it's just off the trail heel.
- When you take your setup, lean into the hill and stay there throughout the swing; don't allow your upper body to work back toward the trail foot.
- Use the same motion you'd use for any other chip shot.
- Make sure you maintain a consistent ratio throughout your swing.

For hardpan:

- Use your less lofted club.
- Move the ball back in your stance so it's just off the trail heel.
- Rotate the clubhead open about 8-10°.
- Lift the handle so the shaft is more vertical.
- Align the ball with the toe of the clubface.
- Use a putting motion.

For deep grass:

- Use your more lofted club.
- Take a wide stance and flare your toes for stability.
- Move the ball back in your stance so it's just off the trail heel.
- Bend your knees so you're sitting nice and low.
- Rotate the clubhead open about 8-10°.
- Make a nice, long swing with a little extra speed.
- Finish with the butt end of your club pointing toward your trail pocket.

Chapter 14

Chipping: A Recap

Once again, I've tossed you a ton of new information. It's game-changing stuff, but it's also a lot to take in.

Revisit chapters as needed. Bookmark the drills you want to find easily and highlight the concepts you'd like to remember. Take time to nail down the foundation and master the swing motion. Then tackle any remaining weaknesses in your chipping game.

I've designed this book to be easy to skim, bookmark, and re-read. And in the interest of making sure you have all the basics in one spot, below is a quick-and-simple recap of everything we just covered.

You can also snag a PDF of this recap at www.VLSCoaching.com/BookOffer.

The Objectives

In every chip shot, you want to meet three objectives:

1. Use the **bounce**—it's your friend.
2. Make contact at a **downward angle.**
3. Choose the **right club** for the job.

Instead of giving yourself several clubs to choose from, select *two* that will be your go-to clubs for chip shots. That will ensure you have more opportunities to practice and master them in a range of chipping situations.

Use your lower lofted wedge when you want less ball flight and more roll. Use a higher lofted club when you're looking for a longer ball flight and less roll.

The Foundation

The perfect chipping setup looks like this:

- Stand with your toes about hip-width apart, heels close together for a slight toe flare.
- Stand close enough to the ball that your chin is just a couple inches from hovering directly over the ball.
- Lean the club shaft toward the ball just slightly and toward the target so that the butt end of the club aligns with the front side of the golf ball.
- Get about 65-70% of your body weight in your lead foot.
- Open the clubface a little.
- Position the golf ball in the center of your heels.

The Motion

A successful swing motion looks like this:

- Get the butt end of the club moving away from the target on the takeaway.
- Rotate the toe open slightly as you swing back.
- Keep the clubhead traveling out in front throughout your swing instead of coming inside and wrapping around your body.
- Let your weight shift with the motion of the club. Start with 65-70% of your weight on the lead foot, slightly shift it to the trail foot on the backswing, and bring it back to the lead foot as you swing through. Finish with most of your weight on the lead foot and your trail heel slightly off the ground.
- At the finish, make sure the butt end of the club is pointing at your belt buckle or slightly in front of it.

The Practice

To stop tilting away from the target and hitting behind the ball, practice the Lead Foot Only Drill:

1. Instead of taking your regular chipping

stance, position your lead foot in line with the golf ball.
2. Balance all your weight on the lead foot, resting the toe of your trail foot on the ground behind you for support. (You can lift the trail foot if you prefer, but I typically recommend using it as a kickstand for the sake of safety and stability.)
3. Hit some chip shots from this position.

To find your rhythm and get better at dancing with the club, practice the Trail Hand Only Drill:

1. Get set up without a golf ball.
2. Hold the club in your trail hand only.
3. Put your lead hand in your pocket.
4. Make a few continuous swing motions back and through.
5. Take a moment to get into the feel of it. Notice the rhythm of the club and your weight moving together back and through, back and through, back and through.
6. Step up to the ball and hit some chip shots.

To find a neutral release pattern that optimizes bounce, practice the Lead, Trail, Middle Drill:

1. Take your regular chipping setup.
2. Take a chip shot and finish with the butt end of the club pointing at your lead pocket.
3. Take another chip shot, this time finishing with the butt of the club pointing at your trail pocket.
4. Take another chip shot, finishing with the butt of the club pointing at your belt buckle. *This is the one you want for almost all chip shots.*
5. Notice how each shot feels in your body and how the ball reacts.

To work on maintaining a consistent radius throughout your swing, practice the Radius Control Drill:

1. Take your regular chipping setup.
2. Take a chip shot, deliberately narrowing your radius as you swing back and through. For example, if you start with 8 inches, you'd narrow it to 4 inches on the backswing, come back to

The Easy Break

  8 as you pass through the middle, and narrow it again to 4 as you finish.
3. Take another chip shot, this time widening your radius on the backswing and follow-through. You might go from 8 inches to 12 inches, for example.
4. Take another chip shot, this time being careful to maintain the same radius throughout your swing. *This is what you want for almost all chip shots.*

To control your angle of attack and improve contact, practice the Low Tee Drill:

1. Tee up the golf ball, but tee it really low. You want it so it's just on top of the ground.
2. Take a chip shot, trying to slightly bump the tee forward
3. If the tee breaks or shifts, tee it back up and try again.

The Mistakes

If you're struggling with distance control:

- Keep the butt end of the club moving away from the target on the takeaway.
- Check to make sure you've got the golf ball in the center of your heels.
- Finish with the butt end of your club pointing at or slightly in front of your belt buckle.
- Work on touch and feel by using the Trail Hand Only Drill.
- Think twice about club selection. Use the less lofted club for more roll and a shorter flight. Use the higher lofted club for less roll and more flight.

If you're having serious contact issues:

- Make sure your upper body isn't rotating backward in the downswing. If it is, practice the Lead Foot Only Drill to kick the habit.
- Keep the clubhead to the outside throughout your swing. Place an

The Easy Break

alignment rod between your toes and the ball as a guide.
- Rotate the toe of your clubface slightly open on the takeaway.

If you can't stop shanking it...

- Make sure you set up closer to the ball than you would for other other shots. Lift the handle a bit so the shaft is even more upright, and only allow for a slight forward shaft lean.
- Keep the clubhead working outside throughout your swing motion. Use an alignment rod as a guide if it helps.
- Finish with the butt end of your club pointing at or slightly in front of your belt buckle.

The Situations

For a downhill lie:

- Use your highest lofted club.
- Move the ball back in your stance so it's just off the trail heel.
- Get closer to the ball and raise the shaft to a more vertical position.

- Make sure the butt end of the club moves away from the ball on the takeaway.
- Maintain a more level, almost putt-like motion.
- In the case of a severe slope, allow the clubhead to move down the slope line as it travels through the impact zone.

For an uphill lie:

- Use your less lofted club.
- Move the ball back in your stance so it's just off the trail heel.
- When you take your setup, lean into the hill and stay there throughout the swing; don't allow your upper body to work back toward the trail foot.
- Use the same motion you'd use for any other chip shot.
- Make sure you maintain a consistent radius throughout your swing.

For hardpan:

- Use your less lofted club.

The Easy Break

- Move the ball back in your stance so it's just off the trail heel.
- Rotate the clubhead open about 8-10°.
- Lift the handle so the shaft is more vertical.
- Align the ball with the toe of the clubface.
- Use a putting motion.

For deep grass:

- Use your more lofted club.
- Take a wide stance and flare your toes for stability.
- Move the ball back in your stance so it's just off the trail heel.
- Bend your knees so you're sitting nice and low.
- Rotate the clubhead open about 8-10°.
- Make a nice, long swing with a little extra speed.
- Finish with the butt end of your club pointing toward your trail pocket.

Notes

Use this space to write any notes of your own. What's your biggest takeaway? What skills or concepts do you want to prioritize in your chipping practice?

Part Three

Bunkers

Welcome to Walt's most dreaded short-game shot. It's Claire's most dreaded shot, too. Even Emily's not wild about them, and we've put in so much bunker practice over the years that she's way more comfortable with them than many of my students.

As for Barry, he's not too concerned about greenside bunkers. He rarely lands in them and at least knows he can get out in one shot. Goes to show you that every golfer is different.

That said, I can confirm that Barry is an outlier. The greenside bunker shot puts the fear of God into many golfers, amateurs and professionals alike. As you'll learn later on, Angela preferred to practice *avoiding* bunkers for much of her LPGA career rather than tackling bunker shots themselves.

It's not just that you're dealing with sand. It's not just that you have to get the ball up over a high lip. It's also the psychological challenge of the bunker.

"You hit a great shot, but then you have a bad bounce, and you're in a bunker," Claire says. "You're *at* the green. You should be *on* the green, but you're not. You're in a bunker. Then it takes you more than one stroke to get out. It just seems like such a waste."

It is a waste. And I won't lie to you: this shot is hard. It takes practice to reach the point where you can approach a greenside bunker with total confidence.

The good news is there's an easier method than the one you've been using. In fact, the VLS approach to bunkers was the reason Claire reached out to me about golf lessons. She found my video on bunker shots on YouTube and saw something there that resonated with her. And now that she's had a chance to learn everything *you're* about to learn, she's able to approach the sand with more certainty.

"I know what to do," she says. "It's just a matter of practice now."

As for Walt, he's having an easier time finding his way onto the green, too. It still takes a couple

The Easy Break

shots to get out of the sand sometimes. But he's steadily getting better at consistently making it out in one.

That's how it is with greenside bunkers. It takes time and practice to build reliable skills. But one of the biggest steps you can take in this aspect of your short game is to simply understand the most critical objective of bunker shots.

And I can pretty much guarantee it's not what you think it is.

Chapter 15

Bunkers: The Objectives

When your ball is in the greenside bunker, you're probably only thinking of one objective.

You want to get that golf ball out of the sand, over the lip, and pray it doesn't run away from the hole when it hits the green.

But you know the drill by now. When you step up to the ball, it doesn't do you any good to obsess over the outcome you're hoping for. That's how you end up banking on the "try anything and hope for the best" strategy.

What you want to do instead is focus on your objectives for the swing itself. What do you need to accomplish with your golf club in order to escape the bunker?

Once again, we're working with three key objectives. And, as always, simplifying your strategy down to these essential intentions is going to make a tough situation feel a lot easier to navigate and much less intimidating.

The Three Objectives of Greenside Bunkers

Objective One: Throw sand onto the green. Highlight this objective. Bookmark it. Type it into your notes app, leave a note for yourself in your golf bag, tattoo it on your hand... do whatever you've got to do to remember that this is the *one* shot where you're not actually trying to make contact with the ball. It's all about the sand.

If you only remember one concept in this entire greenside bunker section, let it be this.
I'll get more specific with this in future chapters, but the basic idea is that you want to take an area of sand around the golf ball and focus on throwing that section of sand up onto the green. Do that, and the sand will take the ball with it.

Objective Two: Use your most lofted club. A higher loft will help you get the ball up in the air and out of the bunker. I personally opt for a 56-degree wedge but a 58 or 60 degree also works.

Objective Three: Control where your clubhead enters the sand and how it moves through. The goal is to enter the sand slightly behind the ball—about 1 to 1.5 inches behind it—and keep the clubhead moving through at a shallow angle. This is very different from chipping, where you're trying to hit slightly down on the ball. For bunker shots, the goal is a shallow strike. If you can master that, you'll see fast improvement in your bunker play.

A Quick Bunker Practice Tip

Now, before we dig into all the strategies that will help you conquer your key objectives, I want to offer a suggestion for overcoming one of the greatest barriers preventing amateur golfers from perfecting their bunker shots.

That barrier is the fact that practicing these shots can be a little scary. Heck, it can feel downright dangerous sometimes.

You're down in the sand, trying to get your ball up onto the green where other people are practicing their putts. You're still learning to control your bunker shots, so, naturally, you worry that you're going to skull one and hit a golfer who's just out trying to work on their green reading skills.

We all know that fear. And it's the reason—or at least one reason—casual golfers tend to avoid practicing this particular shot.

Fortunately, you're about to learn a workaround.

Replace your ball with a golf tee.

Seriously. Lay a tee down on the sand right where your ball would be. You're not planning to make direct contact with the ball anyway, and the sand will carry the tee up onto the green just like it would a golf ball.

You can use this strategy to practice everything I'm about to teach you. And you can feel confident that nobody'll get hurt just because one of your shots was off.

A quick word of warning, though: Many of the practice drills you'll learn in this section also involve drawing lines and boxes in the sand. As you'll find, a little sand art can really help you visualize your objectives and test your progress. But it's not allowed in tournament play. **Intentionally touching the sand with your clubhead before you start your swing is a penalty under the rules of golf.** So be sure to keep those tricks in the practice bunker.

In Short...

- For every bunker shot, you want to achieve three key objectives: throw the sand around the ball onto the green, use your most lofted club, and make sure the club enters the sand just behind the ball and moves through at a shallow angle.
- You can practice your greenside bunker shots using a tee instead of a ball if you're worried about hitting another golfer on the green.

Chapter 16

Bunkers: The Foundation

Getting the ball up over the lip of the bunker is enough of a challenge. When you add in the soft, shifting surface you have to work with, bunker shots get even tougher.

In this chapter, we're building a good, solid base that provides tons of stability as you work to get your ball out of the sand and up onto the dance floor where it belongs. And, as always, you'll learn all the little setup tricks you need to find the proper swing motion and fulfill your objectives without overthinking it.

Don't underestimate the importance of this. The setup might feel like a checklist of nitpicky details, but if you ask Walt which of my tips has made the most significant difference for *his* performance in the bunker, he'll tell you it's this right here—the foundation.

Let's get to it.

Stance

First things first. We gotta get you set up with a solid base that's going to help you hold your own in the sand.

You want a wide stance. **Get your heels about shoulder-width apart, then flare your toes out even wider.**

Once you've got your feet in a solid, stable position, **bend your knees so you're sitting nice and low.** It should feel almost like you're sitting on a short stool.

Finally, this is one time where it's actually better to be a little farther from the ball. Too far is better than too close. As a reference, feel like your arms are extended but not straight or locked (that's *too* much). You want enough space that it feels like you're reaching for the ball a little.

Weight Distribution

Think about loading your weight into your lead thigh. You're going to keep it there for the duration of your swing.

This helps you stabilize your swing motion so you have more control over where the club enters the sand—a key objective in bunker shots, as you may remember.

Clubface

Rotate your clubface open. Don't be afraid to get the club really open to the target line. Remember, this is the one shot where the clubface is not coming in direct contact with the ball, so the open face is okay. It's also going to accomplish two key things for you.

One, it adds even more loft. Between this little trick and the fact that you're using your most lofted club, you'll have a good shot at getting the ball up out of the bunker.

Two, opening the face adds bounce. You need bounce to glide through the sand, similar to the effect you'd want in a chip shot. This maneuver will help you nail that objective of moving the club through the sand instead of digging into it.

Now, the first time you do this, it'll probably feel a little uncomfortable. **You'll look down at your clubface and see it's not aiming anywhere near your target.** *That's fine.* Remember, that open clubface isn't supposed to make contact with your ball, anyway. It's just there to move sand.

Ball Position

The ideal ball position for bunker shots is slightly forward of center.

We're working with sand here, so you can actually make finding the perfect position easier when practicing by drawing a line in the sand that leads straight out from the ball and tracks between your feet. (Note: you are not allowed to touch the sand before hitting the shot in a tournament.) Position yourself so that line is in the center of your stance, then shift back until the line is 2 to 3 inches closer to your lead heel.

Aim

You already know your clubface should be in an open position. But what about your body?

Get your feet, hips, and shoulders all slightly open to the target line—about 8-10°. In other words, if you're a right-handed golfer, you'll open your body toward the left just a bit. If you're left-handed, you'll open toward the right. This position will make it easier to keep your weight in your lead foot and control where the club enters the sand.

The Easy Break

In Short...

- Get a little farther from the ball than you normally would.

- Stand with your heels shoulder distance apart and flared even wider.
- Bend your knees so you feel like you're sitting on a low stool.
- Load your weight into your lead thigh.
- Open the clubface.
- Position the ball slightly forward of center in your stance.
- Slightly open your feet, hips, and shoulders to the target.

Chapter 17

Bunkers: The Motion

For most golfers, the swing motion is the scary part. It's when the moment of truth happens. But I want you to know you've already done most of the work. When you've got the foundation in place and you understand your three objectives, there's really not much more to think about.

In fact, I'd be willing to bet you've been *over*thinking the motion for your bunker shots. All you *really* need to think about are these four simple concepts:

Focus on Throwing Sand

First, you've got to zero in on that objective of throwing sand up onto the green. Instead of swinging to make contact with the ball, swing to throw sand.

Focus on the area of sand around the ball. If it helps, actually draw a small box around the ball. Not too big—about the size of a dollar bill. Your goal is to enter the sand at the front edge of the box and travel through it at a shallow angle, disrupting the entire area and launching it onto the green.

Don't worry about the ball. If you get the sand out of the bunker, the ball will follow.

Keep Your Weight Forward and Your Body Quiet

If you're set up properly, then you've already got your weight forward. We loaded it into the lead thigh, remember?

Now you're just going to keep it there for the entire swing. There's no weight shift. In fact, effective bunker shots are ultimately just arms and hands. There's not much body movement. The more the body moves, the harder the shot becomes. Watch the best greenside bunker players on the tour. You're going to see a steady, quiet body and a *lot* of arms and hands. Your swing should look like that, too.

Swing It Long

When you're in a greenside bunker, you want a good length to your swing. Go ahead and get those arms extended and make a long, free-flowing swing. That length will help you get the sand out of the bunker and onto the green.

Give It a Neutral Finish

Here's a phrase that'll give you flashbacks to the chipping section:

Finish your swing with the butt end of your club pointing at your belt buckle. If you do that, odds are much higher that you've sent the sand—and the ball—right where you wanted it.

In Short...

To create the perfect swing motion for your bunker shots, master these four concepts:

- Focus on throwing a small area of sand around the ball onto the green—don't worry about the ball itself.

Todd Kolb

- Keep your weight loaded into your lead thigh and your body steady throughout the swing.
- Create a lot of length in your arm swing.
- Finish with the butt end of the club pointing at your belt buckle.

Chapter 18

Bunkers: The Practice

You know how it works by now. This is the part where I give you a bunch of drills you can use to sharpen individual bunker skills. And trust me, you won't regret taking the time for this. Ask Emily which aspect of our bunker practice benefited her the most, and she'll tell you it's the hours we put in.

"Honestly, it's something people don't practice very often because they think, 'Oh, maybe I'll only get in one per round and it won't be that big a deal,'" she says. "Then it ends up having a big impact on your round. So I think my dad just getting me in there and making sure I'm getting the reps in was really the biggest help. I would not have done that by myself."

So now I hope you'll let me do the same for you—be that voice in your ear telling you to put in the time.

Remember, you can always practice with a tee instead of a golf ball. Don't let the fear of beaning another golfer keep you from running drills. Just play it safe and lay a tee in the sand where your ball would be.

Now let's get practicing.

Drill #1: Lead Foot Only Drill

What It's Good For:

That's right—the Lead Foot Only Drill is making yet another appearance in your short-game practice strategy. Just as with putting and chipping, this drill will help you maintain a still and steady stance throughout your swing.

In the context of bunker play, the Lead Foot Only Drill is great for correcting a habit of entering the sand too far behind the golf ball. This error is often the result of unnecessary (and unhelpful) body movement. And as you definitely know by now, this drill is one of the most effective ways to train stillness in the body.

The Easy Break

Steps:

1. Step back from the golf ball a bit.
2. Instead of taking your regular stance, position your lead foot in line with the golf ball.
3. Balance all your weight on the lead foot, resting the toe of your trail foot on the ground behind you for support. (You can lift the trail foot if you prefer, but I typically recommend using it as a kickstand for safety and stability.)
4. Make three practice swings from this position.
5. Step up to the ball and make a swing, still balancing on the lead foot only.

Why It Works:

As you've already learned in previous sections, the Lead Foot Only Drill is excellent for training your body to stay steady because there's no other choice. The body instinctively knows that if it leans when you're balanced on one foot, you'll fall.

And if you struggle with entering the sand in the right spot, there's a good chance that the problem is caused by too much body movement. By forcing you to stay steady, the Lead Foot Only Drill is a quick fix.

Drill #2: Line Drill

What It's Good For:

I learned this drill in the late 1980s, and it remains one of my favorites to this day. My college golf coach at UNLV taught it to me.

Like the Lead Foot Only Drill, the Line Drill is great practice for controlling where the club enters the sand. But while the Lead Foot Only Drill helps you develop the skill, the Line Drill allows you to *test* your ability. In fact, **if you're not sure how well you're achieving that goal of entering the sand in the right spot, this ex-**

ercise will answer that question *real* quick.

Steps:

1. Draw a line in the sand. This line is a reference point for where you want to enter the sand.
2. Take your regular setup at the front of the line <u>without</u> a golf ball.
3. Make a swing, trying to enter the sand right at the line.
4. Do a three-setter, scooting back for each swing so you have an untouched section of the line to work with.

5. Hit a real bunker shot and see how it goes.

Why It Works:

By giving yourself an actual, physical guideline, you're able to see where you're disrupting the sand in relation to the line itself. If you're successfully entering the sand right at the line, you'll see it. If you're hitting behind the line, you'll be able to see exactly how far off you are.

This is valuable information as you strategize your greenside bunker practice. Not to mention, it's deeply satisfying to have visual proof when you're right on target. That's the kind of thing that keeps you motivated and assured that all this practice is actually adding up to something.

Drill #3: Box Drill

What It's Good For:

This drill is for throwing sand. I've said it many times before, but I'm going to say it again, because it's *that* important: bunker play is not about hitting the ball the right way. *You're not hitting the ball at all.* This shot is all about throwing sand onto

The Easy Break

the green. The ball just happens to be part of the sand.

If you're having trouble either conceptualizing this idea or making it happen, this is your drill.

Steps:

BOX DRILL OBJECTIVE: THROW SAND AROUND BALL OR TEE

1. Draw a box in the sand. Make it just a little bit wider and longer than a dollar bill.
2. Take your regular setup **without a golf ball.**
3. Make a swing and try to throw the sand inside the box up onto the green.
4. Notice where the sand goes. If you got it up in the air and out of the bunker, odds are, that's where your ball would've gone, too.

Why It Works:

This "throwing sand" thing isn't intuitive for most golfers. We can spend an entire round thinking about almost nothing but making clean, solid contact with the golf ball. Then we land in a greenside bunker where the panic sets in as we wonder what it's gonna take to get this ball out of the bunker and back in the game. Our brains can be a little slow to accept the idea that—all of a sudden—it's not about the ball at all.

The Box Drill forces a shift in focus simply by removing the ball. It allows you to just play in the sand until it feels natural. It invites you to observe what happens to the sand in your bunker shots so you can conceptualize the "throwing sand" idea better. And like the Line Drill, it gives you a chance to evaluate how well you did just by looking at the marks you left on the ground.

Drill #4: Tee Drill

What It's Good For:

This one is more like a practice *approach* than a specific drill. I've mentioned this concept a few times already, but I wanted to include it in this chapter so it remains top of mind when you skim these strategies for your bunker practice in the future.

The Tee Drill is a fix for a common problem when it comes to practicing bunker shots: the ever-present fear that a skulled shot is going to nail an innocent golfer running putting drills on the green.

Steps:

1. Lay a tee on the sand in the spot where your ball would be.
2. Run any bunker drill or take your bunker shot setup and make a shot, treating the tee just as you would a golf ball.

Why It Works:

You can answer this yourself by now. You don't make contact with a golf ball when you're playing a greenside bunker. So it stands to reason that you don't need a ball to practice. You just need a small object that the sand can carry up out of the bunker. A tee is a solid option because it's never going to hurt anybody and you've definitely got a few on you.

I love this fix because it eliminates one of the greatest barriers between golfers and more practice time in the bunker. The other barrier, of course, is that the bunker is an intimidating place full of unpleasant memories and seemingly impossible shots. That's a pretty significant obstacle to overcome, I know. But stick with me because the next two chapters are going to make even the most foreboding bunker feel a lot more manageable.

In Short...

You might feel resistant to practicing your bunker shots for any number of reasons. But these amateur-friendly drills will help you improve your bunker play.

Chapter 19

Bunkers: The Mistakes

Now we get to the *really* fun stuff. It's time to take an up-close-and-personal look at the biggest errors plaguing your bunker play. I'll walk you through the three most common (and disastrous) mistakes casual golfers make. We'll examine which of the three key objectives is suffering in each of these faults and—most importantly—you'll learn what to do to turn things around.

Mistake #1: Extreme Results

You Might Be Making This Mistake If:

- You keep skulling it over the green.

- It's taking more than one shot to get out of the bunker.
- You're thinking of having your mail forwarded to the bunker.

What's Happening:

Maybe you keep leaving it in the bunker. Maybe you're constantly skulling it over the green. Either way, your best efforts are only adding more strokes to your scorecard.

So which objective are we missing here?

Entering the sand in the right spot.

If you're skulling it, you've likely got the low point of your swing too far behind the ball. Instead of creating a shallow strike that travels through the sand, carrying the ball along with it, you're making direct contact with the center of the ball as your clubhead travels back upward.

And if you can't even make it over the lip—let alone airmail the green—it's probably because the clubhead is entering the sand way too far behind the ball. Remember that visualization of throwing the dollar-sized area of sand around the golf ball up onto the green? If you can't seem to get out of the bunker, it's probably because you're working with a *shoebox*-sized area. You're taking way too much sand and ultimately going nowhere.

How to Get Past It:

First, work on stabilizing your upper body. When you keep entering the sand too far behind the ball, unnecessary upper-body movement is the likeliest culprit. As you might remember from the previous chapter, the **Lead Foot Only Drill** is an excellent exercise for eliminating extra movement in the body. It works like this:

1. Step back from the golf ball a bit.
2. Instead of taking your regular stance, position your lead foot in line with the golf ball.
3. Balance all your weight on the lead foot, resting the toe of your trail foot on the ground behind you for support. (You can lift the trail foot if you prefer, but I typically recommend using it as a kickstand for safety and stability.)
4. Make three practice swings from this position.
5. Step up to the ball and make a bunker shot, still balancing on the lead foot only.

You can also use the **Line Drill** to test and sharpen your precision in terms of where the clubhead enters the sand. Here are the steps again so you don't have to go looking for them in the previous chapter:

1. Draw a line in the sand. This line is a reference point for where you want to enter the sand.
2. Take your regular setup on the front of the line without a golf ball.
3. Make a swing, trying to enter the sand right at the line.
4. Do a three-setter, scooting back for each swing so you have an untouched section of the line to work with.
5. Hit a real bunker shot and see how it goes.

Then, when you're out on the golf course, remember to focus your body weight into your lead thigh throughout the entire swing. That's key for stability and will help you avoid slipping into the weight-shift habit that serves you better on iron and driver shots.

Mistake #2: Shanks

You Might Be Making This Mistake If:

- You're hitting shanks in the bunker too often to call it a fluke.

What's Happening:

I know, I know. You *know* what's happening. You're rocketing the ball off the hosel and looking for a sizable rock to crawl under. But what about what's happening in your swing?

Most likely, the clubhead is working too far inside and around your body on the backswing. This causes the heel to be exposed as you swing through, ultimately resulting in a shank.

How to Get Past It:

Now, it's *possible* to not hit a shank when you've got the clubhead working around your body on the backswing. If you manage to release the club correctly as you swing through, you can fix the heel exposure you initially created. But why demand that kind of precision of yourself?

The simpler, better fix is to avoid working the

clubhead to the inside in the first place. The next time you practice your bunker shots, use your club to draw a line along the target line in front of and behind the ball. It should look like the ball is right in the middle of a line tracking directly toward the target.

This is the visual aid for your swing path. **Practice your swing motion, careful to keep the clubhead out towards this line both back and through.**

Get comfortable with this motion and you won't have to worry about accidentally exposing the heel.

The Easy Break

Mistake #3: Poor Distance Control

You Might Be Making This Mistake If:

- Your bunker shots feel good but don't end up where you wanted them.
- You can usually trust yourself to get out of the bunker, but you still don't feel like you're completely in command of the shot.

What's Happening:

You're popping it onto the green, but you don't seem to have much control over the distance the ball travels once it's out of the bunker. Too often, you free yourself from the bunker only to confront daunting lag putts you know will add even more strokes to the hole.

I'll be honest with you: I consider this one more of an advanced skill than an actual error. If you're getting the ball out of the bunker and onto the green consistently, you're already leagues ahead of the typical amateur golfer.

That said, if you *have* reached the level where you're no longer fighting to get it past the lip without overshooting the green, then the inability to control your distance probably *does* feel like a fault to you. It's all relative, right? If you're more of a Barry in the bunker, you might be ready to think about fixing this problem. If you're a Claire, this is an issue for later in your journey as a golfer.

But it's fun to explore either way, so let's get into it.

What might cause this issue?

More often than not, the problem is that you're not being aggressive enough in the bunker. It's a common problem. The bunker has a way of making us immediately imagine all the ways a shot could go wrong. So, without necessarily meaning to, a lot of amateur golfers hold back. They might shorten their swing, slow it down entirely, or take their time on the backswing then come in hot as they swing through. You're likely doing one or all of the above.

How to Get Past It:

The solution is to add length and speed to your swing. But it probably won't be enough to just *do that* the next time you land in a bunker. Remember, this particular bunker error often stems from our fear of the shot. Rather than waiting until that moment of tension to tell yourself what you *should* be doing, start training your body to trust a longer, faster swing now.

The Easy Break

Carve out some time to practice shots from the bunker, focusing specifically on lengthening your swing and adding speed. Go ahead and exaggerate it. If this is hard, slow it down and focus on length first. Once you've got the feel for that, start adding speed. With enough practice, you'll feel more comfortable bringing some aggression to your bunker shots. And I guarantee you'll find it much easier to set yourself up for some good putts, too.

In Short...

If you're constantly skulling it over the green or keeping it in the bunker:

- Practice the Lead Foot Only Drill and Line Drill to improve your ability to enter the sand in the right spot.
- Focus on keeping your body weight in the lead thigh throughout your swing; you don't want any shifting or excessive upper body movement.

If you can't stop shanking it in the bunker:

- Draw a line in the sand that traces the target line both in front of and behind the ball. Practice working the clubhead along this line throughout your swing.

If you're struggling to control where the ball lands once it's out of the bunker:

- Practice adding more length and speed to your swing.

Chapter 20

Bunkers: The Situations

It never feels great to discover that your ball has landed in the rough. Or that you've got to get it out from under the trees. Or that you're gonna have to figure out how to control your roll on a downhill putt.

But nothing gets a golfer sweating like a tough lie in a bunker. I mean, we're talking about taking one of the most challenging shots in the game and making it *even harder*.

I can't promise to make the tricky bunker situations we're about to discuss easy. What I can promise is that you'll unlock strategies that allow you to approach these shots with an actual plan. No more swinging with your fingers crossed and your eyes closed. At the very least, you'll know what you're doing and why. And with a little practice, you may even find that these shots aren't as intimidating as they used to be.

Situation #1: Soft Sand

One thing that makes bunker play particularly challenging is that you can't count on the sand's texture to be consistent bunker to bunker, course to course, day to day. Several factors determine how the sand might work for you or against you, including the specific course you're playing and what the weather has been like.

Sometimes you'll encounter sand that's soft and fluffy, like at the beach. Because there's so much give, you'll find that the clubhead wants to dig down a bit more. To achieve that shallow strike we

The Easy Break

discussed in Objective Three, you'll need to do everything you can to avoid the dig.

First, get the clubface *really* rotated open at setup. You already know that opening the face promotes bounce, reducing dig and allowing the clubhead to glide through the sand. So we want to push this concept even further. Open it up to about 45 degrees.

Then make your swing with the butt end of your club pointing toward your trail pocket as you come through. That'll keep the clubhead lower, helping you get a long, shallow strike through the sand.

Situation #2: Hardpan

Here you have the opposite problem. Instead of fluffy sand, you're dealing with a firm surface. Maybe the rain is packed hard after heavy rainfall. (Wet sand is Walt's greatest nemesis in the bunker.) Maybe there's only a thin layer of sand over tough turf. Either way, it just got a lot more difficult to achieve your objective of throwing sand. So I'm going to say something you haven't heard me say yet in the context of bunker play.

You want to *reduce* bounce so the club can dig into the sand a little. That's what it's going to take to throw sand in this scenario. It will also feel different than fluffy sand, so be prepared for that.

Instead of rotating the clubface open at setup, keep it nice and square. That should give you some dig so you can pick up the sand under the ball. **You still want to get the clubhead entering the sand about 1–1.5 inches behind the ball.**

Now, be aware that the ball will come out lower and roll more than usual when you deliver a square clubface. So adjust your target landing spot accordingly.

The Easy Break

Situation #3: Fried Egg

We all know this stress-inducing scenario. The sand is a little too soft or the ball lands a little too hard. When you walk up to the bunker, you see your ball buried in the sand. It's the dreaded fried egg.

This is another one of those situations where you actually want the clubhead to dig into the sand a little. You're still trying to throw enough sand to carry the ball up onto the green, and to accomplish that, you need the clubhead to go a bit deeper than usual.

So square the clubface at setup to minimize bounce. You might even try closing it a little.

As for the swing itself, treat your backswing as you normally would, but **as the clubhead en-**

ters the sand, keep it working in a more downward strike vs the standard shallow strike we like in a standard bunker shot.

Then shorten your follow-through. What you're going for is more of an explosion shot than a wide, sweeping motion with a big follow-through.

Situation #4: High Lip, Uphill Lie

It's not bad enough that you're in a bunker; you're also on an uphill lie trying to figure out how the heck you're gonna get over a high lip.

I'm not gonna lie. It's a tricky shot. And getting through this situation means thinking through multiple key factors. But don't stress. I'm going to lay it all out for you right now.

First, tilt your shoulders to match the line of the slope, with your trail shoulder lower than your lead shoulder. This helps the clubhead travel along the same angle as the slope, allowing you to control the entry point into the sand and the depth of your clubhead as it moves through.

Now, this tilt will cause the low point of your swing to work backward a little. To overcome that consequence, **move the ball back in your stance. It should be in the center of your feet.**

Rotate the clubface open even more than you usually would for a bunker shot. A 45-degree rotation is about right. As you know by now, this will add a lot of loft and help you get over the lip.

Finally, it's really important that you keep your weight in your lead thigh throughout your swing. On an uphill lie, your instinct will be to let your weight shift into the trail foot. That'll move your low point backward and ruin your shot. Make an active, conscious effort to keep your weight forward.

I wish I could offer you a one-trick fix for this nightmare lie, but I can at least assure you that when you make these few adjustments, you'll have a darn good shot at getting out of the bunker in one.

In Short...

When you're in soft sand:

- At setup, rotate the clubhead open about 45 degrees for more bounce.
- Get the butt end of the club pointing toward your trail pocket as you come through.

When you're on hardpan:

- At setup, square the clubface so it'll dig into the sand a little as you swing through.
- Strategize your shot with the expectation that the ball will fly low and roll out long.

When you're dealing with a fried egg:

- At setup, square the clubface or even close it a little so it'll dig into the sand as you swing through.

- Shorten your follow-through for a more explosive shot.

When you've got an uphill lie and a high lip to get over:

- Tilt your shoulders to match the line of the slope.
- Move your ball position back to the center of your stance.
- At setup, rotate the clubhead open about 45 degrees for more loft.
- Be aware that your weight is going to want to shift back to your trail foot. Focus on keeping your weight in your lead thigh.

Don't Forget!

You can find videos to support the instruction in this book at VLSGolf.com/EasyBreakTips or by scanning the QR code below.

Chapter 21

Bunkers: A Recap

This book contains the simplest, most straightforward bunker play instruction you're going to find. I can pretty much guarantee that. But I want to be honest with you—this particular shot might take a little longer to master than putting and chipping. It's tough. It's unlike any other shot in the game. And (hopefully) you don't get many opportunities to practice it during a regular round of golf.

So make good use of this recap. Bookmark it, copy it into your notes app... whatever helps you find it easily for quick reference the next time you're practicing your bunker shots.

One thing I know for sure: if you put a little time into practicing these concepts, you *will* see progress in your bunker play. Probably more progress than you've seen in all the years you've been golfing. So hang in there. You've got this.

As always, you can even download a PDF of this recap at www.VLSCoaching.com/BookOffer.

The Objectives

For every bunker shot, you want to achieve three key objectives:

1. Throw the sand around the ball onto the green.
2. Use your most lofted club.
3. Make sure the club enters the sand just behind the ball and moves through it at a shallow angle.

You can practice your greenside bunker shots using a tee instead of a ball if you're worried about hitting another golfer on the practice green.

The Foundation

The perfect setup for bunker shots looks like this:

- Get a little farther from the ball than you normally would.

The Easy Break

- Stand with your heels shoulder distance apart and flared even wider.
- Bend your knees so you feel like you're sitting on a low stool.
- Load your weight into your lead thigh.
- Open the clubface.
- Position the ball slightly forward of center in your stance.
- Slightly open your feet, hips, and shoulders to the target.

The Motion

To create the perfect swing motion for your bunker shots, do these four things:

- Focus on throwing a small area of sand around the ball onto the green; don't worry about the ball itself.
- Keep your weight loaded into your lead thigh and your body steady throughout the swing.
- Create a lot of length in your arm swing.
- Finish with the butt end of the club pointing at your belt buckle.

The Practice

To stabilize the upper body and ensure the club enters the sand in the right place, practice the Lead Foot Only Drill:

- Step back from the golf ball a bit.
- Instead of taking your regular stance, position your lead foot in line with the golf ball.
- Balance all your weight on the lead foot, resting the toe of your trail foot on the ground behind you for support. (You can lift the trail foot if you prefer, but I typically recommend using it as a kickstand for safety and stability.)
- Make three practice swings from this position.
- Step up to the ball and make a bunker shot, still balancing on the lead foot only.

To test your ability to enter the sand in the proper place, practice the Line Drill:

- Draw a line in the sand. This line is a reference point for where you want to enter the sand.

The Easy Break

- Take your regular setup on the front of the line without a golf ball.
- Make a swing, trying to enter the sand right at the line.
- Do a three-setter, scooting back for each swing so you have an untouched section of the line to work with.
- Hit a real bunker shot and see how it goes.

To get used to throwing sand, practice the Box Drill:

- Draw a box in the sand. Make it just a little bit wider and longer than a dollar bill.
- Take your regular setup without a golf ball.
- Make a swing and try to throw the inside of the box you drew up onto the green.
- Notice where the sand goes. If you got it up in the air and out of the bunker, odds are, that's where your ball would've gone, too.

Bonus Tip: To practice bunker shots or run any of the previous drills without fear of injuring a golfer on the practice green, lay a tee in the sand where your ball would be. It will behave the same way your ball would since the goal is not to make contact with the ball but to let the sand carry it out of the bunker.

The Mistakes

If you're constantly skulling it over the green or keeping it in the bunker:

- Practice the Lead Foot Only Drill and Line Drill to improve your ability to enter the sand in the right spot.
- Focus on keeping your body weight in the lead thigh throughout your swing; you don't want any shifting or excessive upper body movement.

The Easy Break

If you can't stop shanking it in the bunker:

- Draw a line in the sand that traces the target line both in front of and behind the ball. Practice working the clubhead along this line throughout your swing.

If you're struggling to control where the ball lands once it's out of the bunker:

- Practice adding more length and speed to your swing.

The Situations

When you're in soft sand:

- At setup, rotate the clubhead open about 45 degrees for more bounce.
- Get the butt end of the club pointing toward your trail pocket as you come through.

When you're on hardpan:

- At setup, square the clubface so it'll dig

into the sand a little as you swing through.
- Strategize your shot based on the expectation that the ball will fly low and roll out long.

When you're dealing with a fried egg:

- At setup, square the clubface or even close it a little so it'll dig into the sand as you swing through.
- Shorten your follow-through for a more explosive shot.

When you've got an uphill lie and a high lip to get over:

- Tilt your shoulders to match the line of the slope.
- Move your ball position back to the center of your stance.
- At setup, rotate the clubhead open about 45 degrees for more loft.
- Be aware that your weight is going to want to shift back to your trail foot. Focus on keeping your weight in your lead thigh.

Notes

Use this space to write any notes of your own. What's your biggest takeaway? What skills or concepts do you want to prioritize in your bunker practice?

Part Four

Next-Level Short Game

For LPGA Tour player Angela Stanford, the short game had always been a weakness. And, like many golfers, she preferred to capitalize on her strengths.

She tells the story of the time her college coach announced they'd be working on bunker shots. "I started walking toward the range and my coach said, 'Where are you going?' I told her, 'I'm working on *not* hitting it into the bunker.'"

It's pretty appealing logic; I'll give her that. But now that she's got over two decades of professional golf under her belt—not to mention a major title—she looks back on her reluctance to refine her short game a little differently.

Specifically, she remembers one obstacle she

repeatedly faced in the first major tournament of every season: the tournament now known as the Chevron Championship. It used to be played at the Mission Hills Country Club, where the greens are firm and set up in such a way that just about every shot around the green has to be high and soft.

"I didn't have that high, soft shot," she says. "So when I needed to get up and down to save a par or maybe up and down to make birdie on a par 5, I could never keep that momentum. I always relied on a low bump and run or get it on the ground quick. Now I can hit that high, soft shot around the green. If I'd been able to hit that shot back then, I think my career would've been a little different."

She's talking about a time when she was a younger player at the top of her game. She was driven and committed, with a strong competitive instinct. Not to mention, she was—and *is*—a great ball striker. These qualities had helped her do what few golfers even dare to dream of: sustain a career as a professional player. But to attain that *ultimate* goal of a major victory, she'd have to face her short game.

Angela and I started working together in the fall of 2017. Coaching her has definitely been a career highlight for me. She's an exceptional golfer and an even better human being—kind, warm, funny, and genuine. By the time we met, she would have said her career was winding down. She'd had a few rough seasons and hadn't won a tournament since 2012. But then, she'd also never gotten a handle on the two weakest areas of her game: chipping and putting.

So that's exactly what we focused on. We cleaned up the mechanics of her chip shots. We dialed in her putting. She worked hard to master different types of shots, including the high, soft flop shot she'd been missing on the Mission Hills course.

Then in 2018—her 18th year on tour—Angela Stanford won her first major at The Evian Championship.

"I'd come so close so many different times to winning that first major, and then it was just like, 'Agh, finally!'" she says. "I think improving my short game and winning that major actually extended my career."

Now it's become a joke between us that she *never* goes to the range first. Regardless of what her college coach's experience might have been, *I* see Angela make a bee-line for the putting green or chipping green.

"I've definitely done a one-eighty," she says, "but I love the short game now because I understand it. I have a routine that I can practice and get better at. I think that's why I crave practicing it more."

You've already learned many of the same mechanical techniques that helped shape her victory at Evian and the seasons that followed. Now, in this chapter, I'm going to share the mental and strategic short-game skills that really set a professional like Angela apart. You'll learn how to put your worst shots into perspective, stay relaxed when the stakes are high, create a personalized practice plan, and more.

Even though this is next-level stuff, these insights are accessible to golfers of all levels. In fact, these are the kind of concepts guaranteed to set you apart from your peers, whether you're a beginner, a top-tier player, or somewhere in between.

Let's get to it.

Chapter 22

Proper Expectations

Everyone's journey involves missteps, embarrassments, and failures. If we observe another person at their absolute best and assume we're seeing the whole picture, we're going to get a skewed sense of what the journey "should" look like. We'll set unreasonable expectations for ourselves and get needlessly frustrated when we're actually doing just fine.

This is true in all aspects of life, including—and *especially*—golf.

After all, when we watch ESPN, *all we see* is the highlight reel.

We watch the best players in the world make 25-foot putts, hit 300-yard drives, and nail three-pointers like they could do it in their sleep. It's easy to assume this is simply what golf looks like at the highest level, but I've got news for you:

What you're watching isn't golf. It's just highlights pulled from an 18-hole round full of victories and failures, lucky lies and tricky lies, birdies and bogies.

Don't get me wrong. The players you watch on TV are remarkable golfers. But they're playing the same complicated, unpredictable game you and I are. And just like us, they show up each day with new hurdles to overcome, both on the course and within themselves.

What makes them different from the everyday golfer (aside from the superhuman skill set) is the fact that they know how to set expectations. An amateur player can miss a five-foot putt on the first hole, then waste two strokes trying to get out of a bunker two holes later, and decide that their short game is garbage, they're a rotten golfer, or they're off their game today. Those assumptions are based on extremely limited evidence. Worse, this mindset is pretty much guaranteed to tank a round that wasn't even remotely in trouble yet.

A professional golfer, on the other hand, knows what's normal for someone who plays at their level. They know what they need to achieve in terms of the average distance off the tee or how reliably they should be able to make a fifteen-foot putt. They

The Easy Break

know how many mishits or poorly judged putts they can get away with in a single round.

Because they know these things, they perceive errors as part of the game instead of immediately hitting the panic button. Instead of stressing over the difficulty of the course, they accept hazards as routine challenges that, yes, might *occasionally* trip them up.

Above all, they focus on improving their own game and advancing their own stats instead of getting frustrated because they're not living up to a standard they've set based on someone else's highlight reel.

That's what this chapter is for: helping you reset your expectations based on the average stats for your skill level. Later, we'll talk about the importance of knowing your *personal* averages, which is also essential for setting reasonable expectations and remaining clear-headed during a tough round. But for now, I'm going to offer some guidelines that will help you evaluate different areas of your short game based on what's typical for golfers of your handicap. That way you can more accurately determine where you're struggling and where you're actually doing pretty well.

You'll also see with greater clarity how all these skills you're developing feed off one another. The better you get at lag putting, the less pressure there is on your chipping. The better you get at chipping, the smoother your putting will go. And if you can learn how to find your way out of the bunker in one and follow it up with solid lag putting, you'll be golden.

This is something Angela and I have talked about a lot. As she explains it, "In the past, I'd hit a bad chip shot and I'd say, 'Well, that's a bogie because there's no way I'm going to make that putt.'"

Now that she's worked hard to improve both shots, she doesn't really hit bad chip shots to begin with. "Even if I hit an average chip shot," she says, "in the back of my mind I know my putting's so much better that I can still make this putt. I'm never really out of it."

So let's set some expectations and explore the domino effect of building these skills side-by-side. Use the knowledge you gain in this chapter to focus your practice on problem areas and adopt a more measured, insightful mindset when you're out on the course.

Putting It In Context

At the end of this chapter, you'll find some graphs clarifying the expected outcomes for different types of short-game shots. These graphs are organized by average score. To see the expected outcomes for a golfer at your level, find your average score range, then check out the graph for the shot in question.

You can also get a PDF of this exact same information at www.VLSCoaching.com/BookOffer—that way, you don't have to drag this book along to the golf course.

Before we get into any of that, however, I need to give you a little context. See, I don't want to just set expectations for how well you can expect to perform on the course. I also want to clarify how and when you can expect to see a change in your overall game due to improvements in your short game.

So let's take a look at this shot by shot.

Putting Expectations

Below, you can see the percentage of putts you should be making—based on your average score—from various distances.

You can *also* see I stopped listing percentages for distances greater than 15 feet. This is because at that distance, you're statistically more likely to *three*-putt than one-putt.

That's why I'm constantly preaching the importance of lag putting. Over the course of a round, we'll most often land on the green with much more than 15 feet between our ball and the hole. It's usually more like 25, 30, or even 40 feet. But if you dial in your lag putting, you can turn the looming threat of a three-putt into a clean, easy two-putt, saving yourself several strokes per round.

Chipping Expectations

Now we're going to set some expectations for where the ball is likely to finish in relation to the hole on your chip shots based on your average score and how long the chip shot is.

And as long as we're on the subject, I'd like to set one more expectation.

It's going to take some time before the progress you make in your chipping translates to lower scores.

To clarify why, let's talk about the expectations for professional golfers. For tour players, I have found the gold standard for chipping is seven feet. They want to see their chip shots finish within seven feet of the hole. This is because anyone who plays at that level is going to make a seven-foot putt about 50% of the time. So if they can chip to seven feet and make half of those putts, they're getting up and down half the time. Not too shabby.

Now, let's say you're trying to do the same thing. At first, you're chipping to 15 feet. Then, after refining your technique and putting in a little practice, you're averaging 12 feet. That's a win. No doubt about it—you're making progress.

But it's not enough progress to get you into position for an easy one-putt. You're closer to the hole, but you're making the same number of strokes.

For now. Keep at it, and you'll start closing in—ten feet, eight feet, reaching that threshold where you know that soon, you'll be getting up and down half the time, too.

So don't get discouraged if you start exceeding your own expectations for chipping but your scorecard still looks the same. Stick with it. You'll be rewarded for your hard work eventually, and it'll be very satisfying when it happens.

Bunker Expectations

The stats below are pretty straightforward. They tell you how close you can expect to get to the hole when you're hitting it out of the bunker.

Of course, as I mentioned earlier in the book, managing distance control out of the bunker is an advanced skill. You first need to focus on getting out of the bunker in one shot. And in the interest of setting realistic expectations, I'll tell you right now: that's not going to happen every time. At least, it won't for most golfers reading this book.

So please feel free to use these stats to evaluate

your bunker skills, but also know that **your first and most important goal is to get it out of the bunker and onto the green.** If your bunker shots are currently landing 20-40 feet from the hole, don't sweat it. You can work on closing that distance later. All the more reason to beef up those lag-putting skills in the meantime.

Now, let's take a look at these stats. **Note: The numbers in black refer to the distance between the ball and the pin before you make your shot.**

Average Score: 72-80

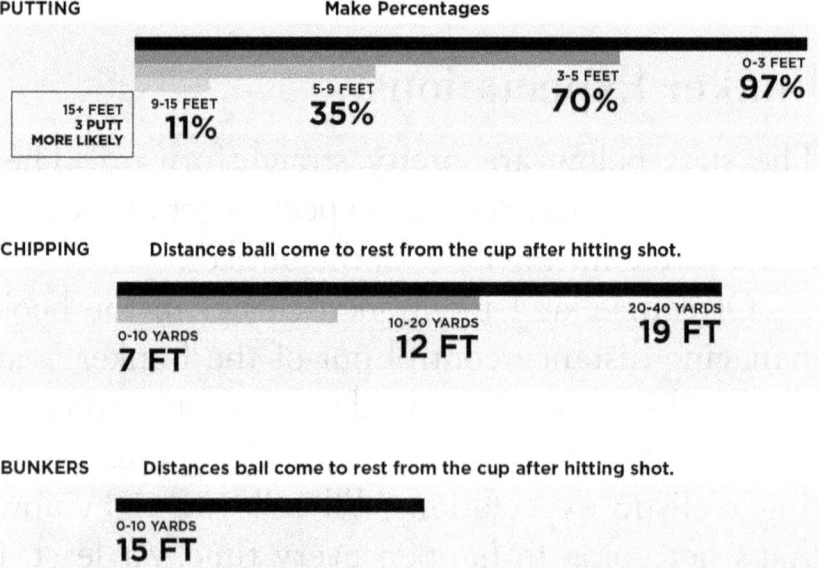

The Easy Break

Average Score: 81-90

PUTTING — Make Percentages

| 15+ FEET 3 PUTT MORE LIKELY | 9-15 FEET 7% | 5-9 FEET 30% | 3-5 FEET 65% | 0-3 FEET 95% |

CHIPPING — Distances ball come to rest from the cup after hitting shot.

| 0-10 YARDS 9 FT | 10-20 YARDS 14 FT | 20-40 YARDS 22 FT |

BUNKERS — Distances ball come to rest from the cup after hitting shot.

| 0-10 YARDS 18 FT |

Average Score: 91-100

PUTTING — Make Percentages

| 15+ FEET 3 PUTT MORE LIKELY | 9-15 FEET 3 PUTT MORE LIKELY | 5-9 FEET 25% | 3-5 FEET 57% | 0-3 FEET 93% |

CHIPPING — Distances ball come to rest from the cup after hitting shot.

| 0-10 YARDS 12 FT | 10-20 YARDS 16 FT | 20-40 YARDS 27 FT |

Todd Kolb

BUNKERS — Distances ball come to rest from the cup after hitting shot.

0-10 YARDS
24 FT

Average Score: 100+

PUTTING — Make Percentages

| 15+ FEET 3 PUTT MORE LIKELY | 9-15 FEET 3 PUTT MORE LIKELY | 5-9 FEET **14%** | 3-5 FEET **55%** | 0-3 FEET **86%** |

CHIPPING — Distances ball come to rest from the cup after hitting shot.

0-10 YARDS **16 FT**   10-20 YARDS **19 FT**   20-40 YARDS **31 FT**

BUNKERS — Distances ball come to rest from the cup after hitting shot.

0-10 YARDS
30 FT

In Short...

When you have the right expectations for your golf game, you can practice smarter and keep a cooler head when a shot doesn't go your way. But for this to work, you have to base your expectations on actual statistics related to your skill level. If you judge your performance based on a highlight reel from

ESPN, you'll only ever be disappointed in yourself and frustrated with the game.

Notes

Now that you know the statistical averages for a golfer at your level, take a minute to consider how this information might influence your practice. Do you see any areas of weakness you can work on? Any opportunities to make up for a shortcoming in one area by leaning into a particular strength? Did you learn any new concepts you want to make sure you remember?

Write your notes here.

Chapter 23

Think Like a Champ

Now that we've established that being a champion doesn't mean pulling off a flawless round or feeling 100% in control at all times, we've got a new question to contend with:

How do exceptional golfers deal with the enormous challenges that are an unavoidable part of this game?

Or perhaps the more important question is: how do the best players in the game overcome the pressure they feel when approaching a tricky or high-stakes shot?

"The biggest hurdle for me personally is that I've always been result-oriented to a fault," Angela says. "I think when I've had my toughest streaks, it's because I've been so tied up in the final result, and you can't do that in golf. The times that I've hit my best, it's more about being in the moment and asking, 'What do I need to do mechanically and mentally to hit this shot?'"

That's why, for champions like Angela, the winner mentality begins with preparation. By the time the tournament begins, she's covered every base, from intensive practice to examining the grass on the course.

"Let's say you're on the back nine Sunday, leading by one, and you miss the seventeenth green," she says. " You have to get into the headspace of, 'I know how to hit this shot. I'm prepared for it.' Once you execute it, it is what it is at that point. But you really derail yourself when you get into the what-ifs. 'What if I hit the wrong club? What if I bogie? What if I hit it in the water?' Those thoughts are really bad."

In this book's previous sections, I laid out solutions for overcoming a range of rattling short-game situations, from chipping on hardpan to navigating a fried egg lie in the bunker. As Angela points out, building your understanding and skill in those shots is the first step to keeping a clear head on the course.

Now, in this chapter, you're going to unlock even more control and confidence by pairing those practical strategies with the mental game of a champion. You'll learn how to ease tension, prioritize your focus, put each shot into perspective, and train your brain to pursue the best possibilities instead of ruminating on your worst fears.

Let's start with the shot-saboteur every golfer knows all too well.

Manage the Tension

Tension is an inevitable part of golf. Heck, it's an inevitable part of *life*. Whether it's a job interview, a tough conversation with your kid, or a six-foot putt on a potential birdie, high-stakes situations have a way of taking over your body, turning you into a jerky mass of tight muscles.

The question is, how does a champ handle tension?

First, they welcome it.

I know it sounds crazy, but consider where tension comes from. You're tense because there's a golden opportunity in front of you. You're on the edge of accomplishing something you care about, whether it's a great job, a deeper connection with your child, or a birdie. The tension you feel in your body is a signal that you're in a state of heightened awareness—that you want something and you've got a real chance at getting it.

So often, we see tension as a sign of fear, but I

want you to embrace it as an indication that you've got an *opportunity*.

Once you've welcomed it, you'll find it's much easier to relax into the moment. Take a second to notice where the tension is in your body. It could be the shoulders, arms, hands... it's different for every golfer, and you'll likely find you almost always hold it in the same place. I feel it in my jaw when I play competitive golf.

After you've done a quick body scan to find where the tension is, make a conscious effort to release it. Let your muscles relax so you can seize your opportunity without seizing up.

Manage Your Focus

Remember what I said four paragraphs ago? How you should view tension as an indication that you have the opportunity to do something great instead of getting caught up in how high the stakes are or ruminating on all the things that could go wrong?

If that tip felt like an "easier said than done" situation, I've got a drill that's going to be a revelation for you. I call it the 1-2-and-3 Drill, and it works like this:

The Easy Break

1. Get set up to take your shot or putt.
2. Look at the target and say, "One."
3. Look at the ball and say, "Two."
4. Take your backswing and say, "And."
5. At impact, say, "Three."

You can also *think* the numbers—you don't have to say them out loud. You don't even have to use those numbers. Use whatever works for you. "One, two, three, four." "A, B, C, D." "Eenie, meenie, miney, moe." It's not about what you say. It's about managing your attention.

If I tell you not to worry about leaving it short or not to think about how close you are to a career round, where's your mind going to go?

Exactly. It's going to get hung up on the very

thought it's supposed to be avoiding. Telling yourself not to think about something is the most effective way to draw attention to it.

The 1-2-and-3 Drill occupies your mind with something else. It helps you focus on just getting the job done—not what it all means in the end—and that's gonna do wonders to ease tension.

Learn to Say "I Will"

One of my favorite questions to ask my students is, "What are you going to do with this next shot?"

I'm not just listening for their strategy. I want to see how they phrase their response. A lot of them begin their answer with "I think."

"I think I'm going to roll the ball over that spot there."

"I think I'm going to use my hybrid."

"I think I'm going to move the ball back a little."

If you've got the mindset of a champion, you're going to answer this question with the phrase "I will."

"**I will** hit my 7 iron at my target."

"**I will** use the higher lofted wedge."

"**I will** lighten my grip."

I know it doesn't seem like much. But after three decades of coaching and all the work I've done on my own mental game, I can attest that this change in phrasing has a drastic effect on the way you perform.

"I will" affirms your confidence, acknowledges the expertise you've gained, and calms your nerves. It commits you to a plan of action and moves you to execute your strategy fully without second-guessing or holding back in case you're wrong.

And if you *are* wrong?

Then you *will* learn from the experience and make an adjustment next time.

It's fine if you need a moment to think through the possibilities, and it's fine if your plan involves a technique you're still trying to master. But when you eventually choose your strategy, trust yourself and commit.

Long Looks at the Hole

The best athletes react to the situation in front of them. They don't spend a lot of time analyzing and calculating and examining their options. They put their focus where it belongs and act swiftly.

Of course, golf isn't like most sports. The ball is stationary. No one's trying to take it from you or knock you down before you can get to it. You've got time to settle in, relax, and focus.

And how do most golfers spend that pause between getting set up and initiating their swing?

They stare at the ball. Instead of taking the athlete's approach of reacting to their present situation, they put most of their focus on the only part of the game that's essentially the same from shot to shot—the little white ball at their feet.

A basketball player doesn't do that when they prepare to shoot a free throw. They focus on the rim. A quarterback looks at the receiver. **In every other sport, we'd instinctively direct our gaze to the target—zero in on where we want the ball to go.** But in golf?

In golf, amateur players glance at the hole or the center of the green or the middle of the fairway, then stare hard at the ball, setting up their aim, clearing their head, visualizing their swing. They might steal another quick look at the target, but for the most part, they're all about the ball.

This is the equivalent of a free throw shooter staring at their hand dribbling the basketball. Just imagine it. Pretty weird, right?

A champion golfer gives their target a good, long look, especially on the putting green, where accuracy is everything. I recommend you do the same.

When you prepare to take a putt, make a few practice motions while looking at the hole. Then you can give the ball a little attention as you get set up and find your aim. Before you initiate the takeaway, look at the hole one more time. Then return your focus to the ball, make the stroke, and calmly watch the ball roll toward the cup.

Play Your Averages

Know your stats. It's one of the most reliable ways to keep a cool head when things go sideways in the middle of a round.

Let me illustrate this by going back to that free throw shooter. Let's say they know for a fact that, historically, they've made 90% of the free throws they've attempted. If they miss the first two free throws in a game, they're not going to panic. Neither will their coach. They won't change anything or try a new technique because they know that, statistically speaking, missing a couple shots is completely normal and they're likely to make the next several they attempt.

The best golfers analyze their game the same way. **They look at how they perform over a long period of time.**

What percentage of five-foot putts did you make in the last season? How often were you able to get out of the bunker in one? How close to the hole do your chip shots land, on average? When you know the answers to questions like these, you're less likely to overreact and overcorrect when a shot doesn't go your way.

Not only does this insight help you keep a cool head, but it also helps you decide when to take risks and when to play it safe.

"When I get into high stress situations, I weigh my options," Angela says. "First off, what shot is the perfect shot? How comfortable do I feel doing that right now? Maybe it's later in the tournament and I'd rather hit a different shot to give myself a putt for par, whereas early in the week, if I'm on the second hole, I may try to pull off the big lob shot."

So I encourage you to do what a champ would do and get a clear understanding of your big picture—your historical data. Know your averages so you don't react based on one or two shots or even one round.

State the Facts

Routines are the secret to success. You've probably learned this yourself as you've navigated both your personal and professional lives.

In my case, I start everyday by packing a lunch, grabbing a banana, and heading to the gym. After getting some fitness in, I have an apple and go to work. Just a series of small, consistent actions that boost my energy and get me in the right headspace

The Easy Break

to enjoy a productive day. And because it's always the same, I do it on autopilot. I don't have to talk myself into going to the gym or decide what to eat. I'm not using up mental energy or willpower. I don't have to summon motivation. I simply follow a system I've built—a system that preserves my energy and gets me started on the best possible path.

Champion golfers do the exact same thing on the golf course. **They have a routine they execute with every single shot they take.** This routine helps them evaluate the situation and strategize their response automatically.

The routine I use—and the one I teach all my students to use—is called "State the Facts." It's exactly what it sounds like.

When you approach any shot, state the facts to yourself. What key information do you have about the situation you're in?

Look at things like the length of the shot, the conditions of the wind, if it's an uphill or downhill lie, the placement of the pin... any details you need to know to strategize your next move. For example, you might approach a putt saying, "Okay, it's 14 feet, slightly uphill, and breaks to the right."

Once you've stated the facts, state the action you will take. Remember, we're looking for an "I will" statement. "I will roll the ball over that little bald patch."

Then end with a positive affirmation. You might think to yourself, "I'm gonna make this putt." Or you might just allow yourself to smile a little bit or take a calming breath and relax.

That's the routine: facts, action, affirmation. Do this with every shot and I guarantee you'll find yourself sliding into a system of strategizing that's defined by ease and confidence instead of whirling thoughts and growing dread.

In Short...

To approach your short game with the mentality of a champ:

- Notice where you're holding tension in your body and consciously relax those muscles.
- Use the 1-2-and-3 Drill to focus your attention on something productive throughout your swing or putting motion.
- State your strategy using "I will" statements instead of "I think."
- When you prepare to take a shot, put

most of your visual focus on the target rather than the ball.
- Be aware of your historical averages so you can put minor errors into perspective and avoid unnecessary adjustments.
- Approach each shot with a routine of stating the facts, stating your plan of action, and offering yourself some affirmation.

Notes

Did anything you learn in this chapter change the way you think about your approach to the game? Did you learn any new concepts you want to make sure you remember? Write your notes here.

Chapter 24

Practice Plans

"If you talk to champions when they win golf tournaments, they never just say, 'I got lucky today.' Yeah, they might have gotten a good break, but they knew how to hit that shot because they've been doing it for the last however-many-years of their life *on purpose*. And *on purpose*, I have a specific routine for my short-game practice. That's where the championship mindset starts."

Angela is absolutely right. Practicing is a skill in and of itself, and it's a skill that's all about deliberate choices and routines. There's an art to turning a technique into a habit and a habit into progress.

Most amateur golfers assume any kind of practice is good practice. They'll show up on the practice green, roll a bunch of putts, maybe see a little improvement, and figure they've taken a solid step forward in their game. The next time they're on the course facing the much more complicated realities of an actual round, they won't see much evidence of the work they put in. They'll run up against the same limitations, experience the same frustrations, and end up with the same scores.

Randomly hitting a ball around the practice green is *fun*, and that certainly counts for something. But this try-whatever approach to short-game practice is *not* the formula for a noticeably better game.

You're actually about to discover the formula. I'm sharing three practice plans carefully designed to ensure you see real progress not just on the practice green but in an actual round. The routines you're about to learn all have a few essential things going for them.

First of all, they're *tight*. You'll get to choose between 35- and 60-minute practice plans. I've calculated the time you'll need down to the minute so you can choose the one that works for your lifestyle. Fit a practice session in on your lunch break or before or after work. Squeeze in some exercises before breakfast or while your spouse watches that show you don't like.

The entire point of this book is to provide solutions that actually work for the everyday golfer, and that means offering practicing plans that fit into the everyday golfer's life. I know you love golf. But I also know your world probably doesn't revolve around the game. So I want to equip you with resources that will help you play your best without demanding too much of your time. Heck, even Angela says:

"I used to be overwhelmed by short-game practice. I just thought, 'I'm never going to fully understand this, so I'm frustrated by it. I don't want to work on it.' But the more I learn, the more I realize I don't need to be out here all day. I need to focus on my fundamentals from my instructor and just work on it a little bit each day."

You'll also notice that these practice plans touch on all aspects of the short game, including drills for putting, chipping, and bunker shots. Another bad practice habit amateurs tend to have is focusing on only one type of shot. Having coached players of all skill levels for thirty years, I can say for a fact that you'll see the most overall improvement in your game when you drill a variety of skills in each practice session. As we discussed in the Proper Expectations chapter, all these shots are interconnected. If you want to improve your seven-foot putts, by all means, practice your seven-foot putts. But remember that better lag putting, chipping, and bunker shots all set you up for more success on those short putts, too.

For each type of shot, you'll see what I call Cornerstone Drills listed in bold. These exercises help you hone essential skills for mastering the concepts you learned in this book. I encourage you to run Cornerstone Drills every time you practice your short game. There's also time built in to work on whichever drills stand to help you the most right now. You'll see an index at the bottom of the practice plans referencing all the exercises you've learned in this book.

Rather than printing these plans in a book that'll be inconvenient to carry around, I've made them available in a downloadable PDF. Visit www.VLSCoaching.com/BookOffer to access your practice plans.

Follow these plans, and you'll definitely see some exciting improvement over time. These are the best techniques I know for advancing your short game, lowering your scores, and finding more confidence as you approach the green.

Bring a positive spirit to your practice, and you'll even have fun along the way. Sharpening your short game may not offer the same thrill as, say, blasting it off the tee at the driving range. But it's easier on your body and one of the most reliable ways to swiftly lower your scores. If that's not a formula for fun, I don't know what is.

In Short...

The next time you head to the practice green, bring one of these practice plans with you. They're designed to fit your schedule and strategized to help you improve your game in meaningful ways. If you opt to create your own routine, remember that it's better to drill multiple short-game skills rather than focusing on a single one for an entire practice session.

Chapter 25

Testing

Do a quick mental audit of your short-game practice. Are the shots and putts you set up all a little too tidy? Too simple? Too consistent?

It's a habit most amateur golfers fall into. They get so focused on drilling the motion they don't realize they're also repeating the *circumstances* of the shot. They're always the same distance from the cup and always chipping from a level lie. Then they get frustrated when the improvement they see on the practice green doesn't translate to lower scores in an actual round.

Elite golfers don't just drill their skills under ideal conditions. **They work with different**

lies on different surfaces and different slopes, and that's how they test what they're *really* capable of. That's how they determine their averages and get a clearer idea of what they need to do to advance their short game.

You're about to follow the same strategy. In this chapter, you'll learn my favorite tricks for testing where you *actually* are in terms of putting, chipping, and bunker shots.

This form of practice might be slightly more challenging than what you're used to, but it will also be more effective, more informative, and a whole lot more interesting.

Test Your Putting With the Completion Drill

You don't need me to explain that you rarely get to putt on a flat surface in a typical round of golf.

The Easy Break

And yet, when most casual golfers practice, they hit the same putt over and over: an 8-10 foot putt on the flattest part of the green. In my 30 years as a coach, I must have seen it half a million times.

For a clearer understanding of where you *really* stand with your putting, do the Completion Drill. Here's how it works:

The Completion Drill

1. Look at your Putting Expectations chart and decide what you want to work on. Let's say, for example, you're scoring in the nineties and want to test your averages on those 5-9-foot putts.
2. Place five balls around the hole in a circle at varying distances between 5 and 9 feet.
3. Putt each ball one by one, then check how your results compare to your Expectations chart. If you're scoring in the nineties, you should have made about 25% of those putts.
4. If time allows, run the drill again. This allows you to roll 10 putts, which gives you a larger data set and a more accurate average.

This drill should give you a good variety of putts, allowing you to practice putting downhill, uphill, and over different breaks. Run this drill for every range on your chart: 0-3 feet, 3-5 feet, 5-9 feet, and 9-15 feet. It's also a good idea to practice putts 20-30 feet out and see how many of them you can two-putt.

Keep track of your stats to see how well your performance stacks up and get a clearer sense of what you can expect from yourself during an actual round of golf.

Test Your Chipping With Five Balls

Once again, we want our practice to reflect the variety of lies and situations that confront us during a real round. To test your chipping skills accurately, take five balls and toss them on the ground.

Ideally, you'll end up with a variety of lies. You

might get a few good ones. Maybe one lands in a hole. Another might be in the long grass. You get the idea.

Play all five shots to the same hole. Once you've hit every ball, take a look at where they all finished. Find the ball that's the third closest to the hole. That's where your "average chip" shot finishes.

Do this routine a few times, and be sure to repeat it under different circumstances with different clubs. Practice on an uphill slope, on a downhill slope, and out of the rough. Walt likes to make a game of it—see if he can get all of them within three feet.

Each experiment will show you what your average outcome looks like, and that knowledge will help you establish clearer goals, set better expectations, and go into your next round a little wiser.

Bunker Practice With Five Balls

You know where this is going.

To practice your bunker shots, you're going to toss five balls into the sand. Hit all five, then check the green to find the one that's the third closest to the hole. That's your average.

Once again, you can use the stats I provided in the Proper Expectations chapter to gauge your performance. But bear in mind that bunker shots aren't the same as chip shots. Many amateur golfers aren't ready to worry about how close they can get to the hole. Right now, it might be enough to just get out of the bunker. In which case, I'd also encourage you to note what percentage of your bunker shots end with the ball on the green—*anywhere* on the green.

Just like with the chip shots, repeat this exercise in different areas of the bunker to get a fuller under-

The Easy Break

standing of how you're likely to perform in a range of bunker scenarios. Carry that knowledge with you to the golf course and enjoy the confidence that comes with proper expectations and a clear plan for improvement.

In Short...

No two shots are exactly alike in the game of golf, and you won't fully grasp your true short-game capabilities until you've tested and practiced your skills in a variety of situations. Instead of drilling the exact same shot over and over again, try this:

- For putting, position five golf balls around the hole at varying distances and see how many you can sink.

- For chipping, toss five balls onto the ground and chip them onto the green from wherever they land. The third closest ball to the hole represents your average.
- For bunker shots, toss five balls into the sand and play each of them from the position where they come to rest. The third closest ball to the hole represents your average, though it might be enough to evaluate your bunker play based on how reliably you can get onto the green at all.

Chapter 26

Next-Level Short Game: A Recap

I hope at this point you're feeling wiser, more prepared, and truly inspired to put these concepts to work in your golf game. It's one thing to know the physical techniques that ensure successful short-game shots. When you can pair that technical insight with a champion's mentality, you'd better believe you'll start seeing faster, more sustainable progress than ever before.

As always, I'd like to close out this section with a quick cheat sheet for easy reference in the future. Turn to this recap anytime you need a refresher on the information you just learned. Visit www.VLSCoaching.com/BookOffer for the PDF version.

Todd Kolb

Proper Expectations

To strategize your practice wisely and keep a cool head on the course, you need to approach your game with proper expectations. Often, what we think we *should* expect of ourselves isn't in line with the actual averages for golfers playing at our level.

This data can help you put things into perspective:

Average Score: 72-80

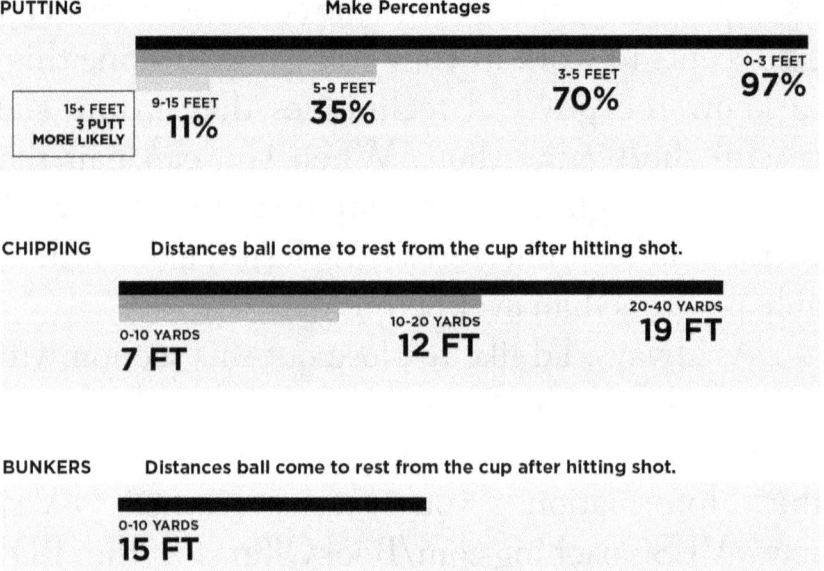

PUTTING — Make Percentages
- 15+ FEET: 3 PUTT MORE LIKELY
- 9-15 FEET: 11%
- 5-9 FEET: 35%
- 3-5 FEET: 70%
- 0-3 FEET: 97%

CHIPPING — Distances ball come to rest from the cup after hitting shot.
- 0-10 YARDS: 7 FT
- 10-20 YARDS: 12 FT
- 20-40 YARDS: 19 FT

BUNKERS — Distances ball come to rest from the cup after hitting shot.
- 0-10 YARDS: 15 FT

The Easy Break

Average Score: 81-90

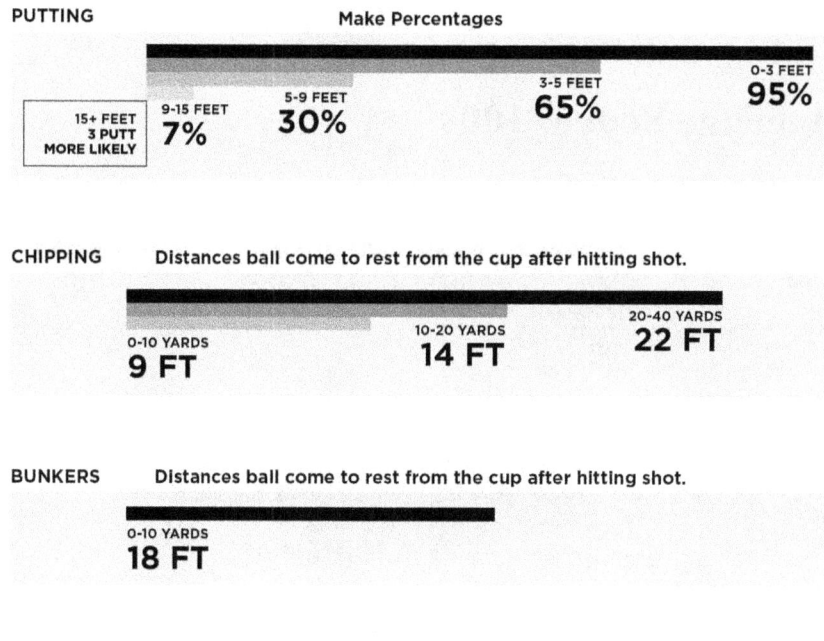

Average Score: 91-100

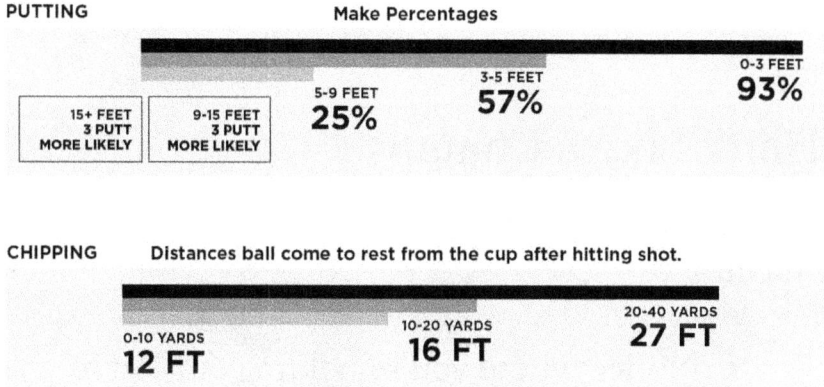

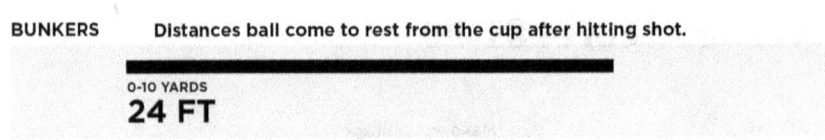

Average Score: 100+

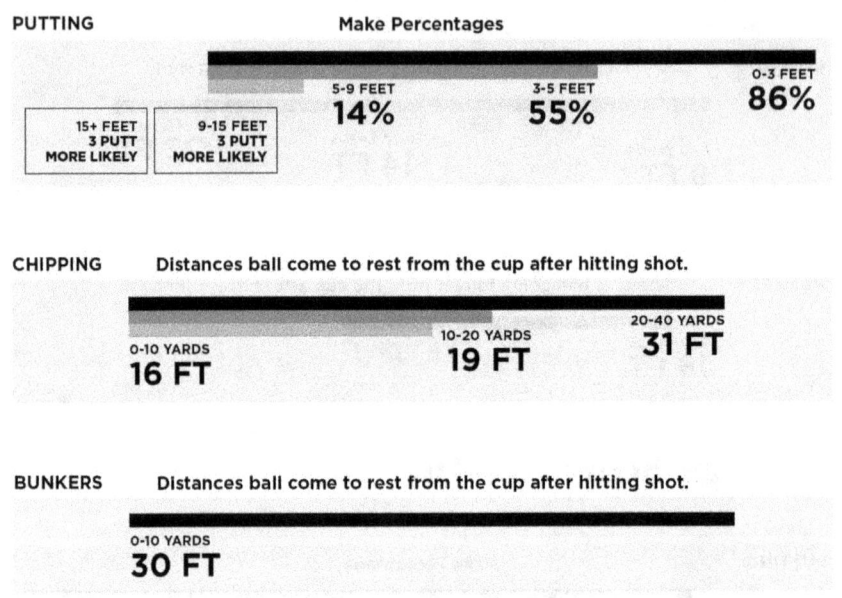

Think Like a Champ

To approach your short game with the mentality of a champ:

- Notice where you're holding tension in your body and consciously relax those muscles.

- Use the 1-2-and-3 Drill to focus your attention on something productive throughout your swing or putting motion.
- State your strategy using "I will" statements instead of "I think."
- When you prepare to take a shot, put most of your visual focus on the target rather than the ball.
- Be aware of your historical averages so you can put minor errors into perspective and avoid unnecessary adjustments.
- Approach each shot with a routine of stating the facts, stating your plan of action, and offering yourself an affirmation.

Practice Plans

You don't have to dedicate countless hours to your short-game practice. In fact, *how* you practice has much more bearing on your success than the amount of time you put in. To see meaningful results:

- Practice consistently, even if you have to keep your sessions short.

- Focus on a variety of short-game shots.
- Focus on essential fundamentals as well as improving in your areas of weakness. Visit www.VLSCoaching.com/BookOffer to download practice plans strategized for success.
- Bring a positive attitude to the practice green. It helps more than you might think.

Testing

No two shots are exactly alike in the game of golf, and you won't fully grasp your *true* short-game capabilities until you've tested and practiced your skills in a variety of situations. Instead of drilling the exact same shot over and over again, try this:

- For putting, position five golf balls around the hole at varying distances and see how many you can sink.
- For chipping, toss five balls onto the ground and chip them onto the green from wherever they land. The third closest ball to the hole represents your average.
- For bunker shots, toss five balls into the sand and play each of them from the

The Easy Break

position they landed in. The third closest ball to the hole represents your average, though it might be enough to evaluate your bunker play based on how reliably you can get onto the green at all.

Notes

Use this space to write any notes of your own. What's your biggest takeaway? What skills or concepts do you want to incorporate into your short game going forward?

Chapter 27

The Next Era of Your Golf Game

As we know, Barry got his first eagle decades ago. His younger years as a golfer gave him that memory of his dad plowing up the hill to witness his son's success, plus plenty of other memories of hard-fought tournaments and an enviably low handicap. But what I'm most curious about is who he is as a golfer *today*... and where he sees his game in the future.

"A couple weeks ago, I played a nine-hole course nearby," he says. "It's a par 33—not a full par 36—and I made nine pars but hit only one green in regulation. And it's funny, I wasn't that familiar with the golf course, and I hit to the wrong green on one hole. Of course, I had to drop off the green. It was about 50 yards to the correct green, and I got *that* up and down. I mean, it was just one of those days. I hit *one* green and made *nine* pars. And that's all because of this instruction."

Walt says his golf partners have noticed a change in his game, too.

"They see my good games, and once in a while, they see my bad games," he says. "But the friends I've golfed with for years—they've definitely seen the improvement."

As for Claire, she's now equipped with the tools she needs to approach golf with the same clarity and dedication that made her such a strong tennis player.

"My scores have improved," she says. "I'm still a high handicapper, but just having the form and consistency is going to pay off in the end. My goal is to keep playing and enjoying the game for many years. I do hope to start breaking 100, and I do think that's going to come soon."

Thanks in part to Emily's lifelong dedication to the short game, she's already well on her way to achieving her biggest golf goal: scoring in the seventies consistently. As for her future in the game, she says:

"I love playing college golf, especially at a smaller scale, but after college, I want to play more just for fun. I might join a little women's league. I

The Easy Break

like just having fun with it and not putting so much pressure on it."

And Angela? She's finishing her final year on the LPGA tour as I write this, but just like the rest of us, the drive to play at the top of her game can't be dampened by a life transition. "I wouldn't still be here if I didn't want to win one more time," she says.

Whatever you want out of this game—whether it's breaking 100 or breaking 80, keeping up with your grandkids or competing in tournaments, visiting the world's golf courses or simply enjoying the challenge of consistently beating the golfer you were yesterday—your goals are attainable.

If you take anything away from this book, I hope it's that.

The beauty of golf is that it's *always* your game. Don't ever let age, overcomplicated golf tips, or even short drives let you believe you have to settle for declining scores and a less enjoyable time.

Put the concepts in this book to work, and I can promise you, you'll be challenging yourself, surprising yourself, and creating new memories on the golf course for years to come.

Free Bonus (Because You're an Insider Now)

Thank you for purchasing *The Easy Break* and trusting me to be your guide as you work toward your own short-game breakthrough. I love helping golfers discover what they're truly capable of. It's my mission, my joy, and the entire reason I've chosen to spend 30 years in this career. And I can't do it without golfers like you inviting me to share what I know.

To show my gratitude, I'd love to offer you a few exclusive perks.

First, I've got a bonus chapter you're gonna want to see. This Lost Chapter didn't make it into this book, but it probably should have. It's where you'll learn how to pull off major short-game feats like the super flop shot, the 40-yard bunker shot, and overcoming the dreaded yips.

Get the chapter at www.VLSCoaching.com/BookOffer or scan the QR code on the next page.

If you're ready to take your game to the next level with one-on-one coaching or a customized coaching program, send us an email at Info@VLS-Golf.com.

As you may have learned from Walt, Claire, Barry, and Angela, the VLS System has become more than a golf technique for a lot of our students. It's a mindset and a community. And as far as I'm concerned, you're one of us now.

So I hope you'll take advantage of these insider perks. The deeper you dive into the world of VLS Golf, the more you'll get out of this game.

I can't wait to hear what you do with the things you learn.

Acknowledgments

Bringing my short-game instruction to a wider audience in the form of a book is definitely a dream fulfilled for me. And it's a dream I wouldn't have been able to fulfill on my own.

    First and foremost, I'd like to thank my wife Susan, who began this journey with me thirty years ago when we started a golf academy with a twelve thousand dollar loan from a relative. I'm so proud of what we've built, and I wouldn't be the instructor I am today without her unwavering support. I'm also grateful to my daughter Emily, who kindly agreed to be featured in this book and whose tenacity and commitment to the short game has enabled her to excel even when the deck seemed stacked against her at times. Finally, thank you to my son JT, who's now a member of our crew and generously shares his own passion for the game with Walt, Claire, Barry, and all our other VLS Golf students. We are better with him on our team.

    As always, I owe a debt of gratitude to my VLS

Golf team. Every piece of content I've put out over the last fifteen-plus years has Nick Anson's fingerprints on it, and the work is better because of it. Nothing I've produced, including this book, would have been possible without his insight. I'm grateful for his dedication to our mission and his trust in me. I also owe a huge thank you to Jordan Knowlton, who serves as the bridge between me and the everyday golfer. He keeps the wheels turning on the back end, making sure our team and the information we provide are always easily accessible to our golfers.

I'd also like to thank Abi Wurdeman, whose talent for storytelling and communication have made it possible for me to share my instruction on the page in a way that resonates with readers. I'm grateful to her for capturing my message and mission with authenticity.

This book wouldn't be the accessible guide that it (hopefully) is without the design skills of Jerrice Thorson. From crafting a beautiful cover to turning complex information into engaging graphs and downloadable resources, she's managed to create a visual experience that exceeded my hopes for this book.

And, of course, *The Easy Break* wouldn't have been the same without the voices of our golfers. Not only have Walt, Claire, and Barry generously donated their time and insight through interviews, but they've also offered readers of this book something I can't: the firsthand perspective of an everyday golfer who's turned this instruction into a renewed love for the game.

I'd also like to extend a massive "thank you" to Angela Stanford, who took time to contribute her own thoughts to this project while on tour. I'm so grateful to include her invaluable insights in this book and even more grateful to have had the opportunity to coach her in the first place. Having someone trust you with their career is a tremendously powerful thing, and taking this journey with Angela has been one of the highlights of my professional life.

Finally, I'd like to thank you, the everyday golfer, for continuing to inspire my work. Your passion and commitment to the game are what drive me. Thank you for allowing me to play a role in your evolution as a golfer.

www.ingramcontent.com/pod-product-compliance
Lightning Source LLC
Chambersburg PA
CBHW050855160426
43194CB00011B/2159